Jacques Torres'
A YEAR IN
CHOCOLATE

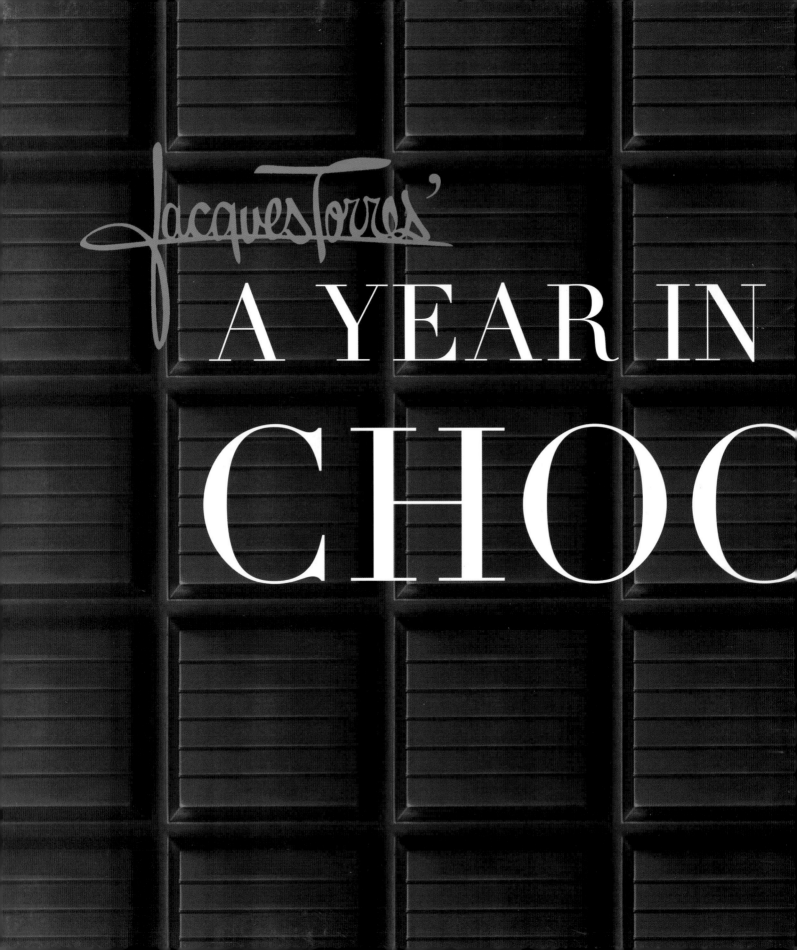

Jacques Torres'

A YEAR IN
CHOC

OLATE

JACQUES TORRES

PHOTOGRAPHS BY STEVE POOL

STEWART, TABORI & CHANG

New York

Published in 2008 by Stewart, Tabori & Chang
An imprint of Harry N. Abrams, Inc.

Library of Congress Cataloging-in-Publication Data

Torres, Jacques.
    Jacques Torres' a year in chocolate / by Jacques Torres with Judith Choate.
       p. cm.
    ISBN 978-1-58479-642-8
    1. Cookery (Chocolate) 2. Chocolate desserts. 3. Holiday cookery. 4. Year. I. Choate, Judith. II. Title.
III. Title: Year in chocolate.
    TX767.C5T675 2008
    641.6'374 — dc22
                                    2008009186

Editor: Luisa Weiss
Designed by Joel Avirom, Jason Snyder, and Meghan Day Healey
Blackboard illustrations by Jason Snyder
Production Manager: Jacquie Poirier

The text of this book was composed in Linotype Didot

Printed and bound in China
10 9 8 7 6 5 4 3 2 1

HNA
harry n. abrams, inc.
a subsidiary of La Martinière Groupe

115 West 18th Street
New York, NY 10011
www.hnabooks.com

ACKNOWLEDGMENTS

It would seem to be good enough fortune just to be in the chocolate business, but we are blessed to have an amazing array of very close friends who love and support us in everything we do.

This company started with the spark of an idea and grew into a dream-come-true thanks to unending commitment, dedication, and a lot of hard work. The business partnership is all the more incredible because it is based on a shared love that simply cannot be rocked off its base. We are so lucky to have this bond, to live this dream, and to share these moments. A year in chocolate: who knew what a year it would be!

To Maman/Louise: Vous êtes la source de tout l'amour. Merci de partager votre coeur. Bisoux bisoux.

Louis and Arlette Franchain: Avec tout mon coeur — bisoux, bisoux, bisoux (et merci).

Judie Choate is a gift to behold and to cherish. Thank you for all you did to navigate the bumps along the way with grace and a never-ending and endearing friendship.

Thank you to Stephen Pool, photographer extraordinaire — a deep well of both talent and emotional fortitude. You are a true treasure, my friend.

The collective JTC/JTA/JTR staff members past and present: Thank you to all of you.

Sottha Khunn, Mark Fradin, and Scott Cohen: You are truly the brothers of this family. Your support, love, friendship, and expertise are treasured and appreciated. Sending you lots of love.

Glenn Dopf: Big Brother, for all you do, all the time, without reservation, with immeasurable passion and joy. Words cannot express the gratitude for the depth and breadth of your friendship.

John and Linda Kuipers: No words can express the appreciation that exists for your love. You set the example for all that is good in human nature.

To Birgitt Stepanow Adams, Karen Coley Huddleston, Bea Flammia Burton, and Laura Fastie Graphsi: Your core values and unfailing support make all things not only possible, but a joy. You make each rise and fall on the roller coaster ride of life a positive experience. Nobody can find the sense of humor in any situation like you — thank you for that.

Rebecca Lessard: You've given the concept of soaring a whole new definition. You are truly the wonder in Wings of Wonder. Thanks for unzipping the privacy bag and making sharing a wonderful thing.

Rob Brofman and Betty TWD: You were there every step of the way, asking the hard questions, shining the spotlight into every corner, looking for the monsters in the closet. You are true friends.

Dorothy Cann Hamilton: Words do not exist that would capture all of the loveliness, generosity, and intelligence that makes you who you are. Thank you seems inadequate, but you know it comes from the bottom of the heart.

To the Girls Who Just Want to Have Fun: Jeanne Caldie, Marianne Cornellier, Vivian Dion, Kathy Guttenberg, Anne Havill, Marie Hooper, Linda Kuipers, Lee Miller, Helen Rataj, Madeline Robinson, Jana Rockne, and Patty West: Thanks for the warm welcome, the open door, and the cozy circle of friendship with which you embraced me . . . and for being the private tasting panel!

Hasty: Your patience and understanding is deeply appreciated.

Montana Man: You've colored everything with the most remarkable hue and then you seasoned it with cbs moments. Deeply touched. Forever grateful. Somewhat lucky.

Kris: Without you, there would be no book. There is no way that we can thank you for your support, understanding, and care. From Jacques: Throughout the building of Jacques Torres Chocolate through the last correction on this book and onward. From Judie: Your trust in my ability to deliver the book that would best express a year in chocolate is deeply appreciated. You are the best!

CONTENTS

INTRODUCTION

From the moment I stepped into a pastry kitchen at the age of fifteen, I have had a fascination with chocolate. To me, it is an absolutely magical food. You can eat it, drink it, mold and sculpt it. It can be bitter or sweet; solid or liquid; white, milky brown, or deep, dark brown. It is sensual to work with and to savor. And it is good for you to boot! In a word, nothing in the world is quite like chocolate.

Throughout my career as a pâtissier, I developed skills and formulated my own techniques for creating visually exciting, yet still delicious confections. All the while I was learning more about chocolate. I traveled to the countries where it is cultivated and met with growers, including small farmers in Africa and the Caribbean. I searched out as many different types of cacao beans as I could find, and I tasted the finest chocolates made by the world's best chocolatiers. Slowly, through the years, chocolate went from being a fascination to a passion.

I loved my work in the pastry kitchen, but when it came time to strike out on my own, chocolate was the answer to my dream of opening my own business. Everybody loves chocolate, so it seemed an obvious choice, plus it would give me the opportunity to continue to grow creatively as I learned more about the manufacture of fine chocolates. Also, a chocolate shop would allow me to live a more balanced life than the long, long hours of restaurant work would. Finally, scientists were beginning to report on the health benefits of chocolate, something that only added to its desirability.

I discovered the space for my shop in an out-of-the-way, rather desolate neighborhood in Brooklyn now called Dumbo (an acronym for "down under the Manhattan Bridge overpass"). Of course, desolate neighborhoods typically mean affordable rents, which are perfect for jump-starting a new business. Fortunately, the neighborhood did not stay desolate for long. New York City's booming real estate market has turned Dumbo into a desirable area with plenty of residential lofts, lots of unused commercial space, and an easy commute to Manhattan.

With my partners, Kris Kruid and Ken Goto, I designed and built (yes, we actually donned overalls and picked up hammers and saws) the Brooklyn shop. I wanted it to have the same feeling as the tiny neighborhood pâtisseries of France that offer a friendly welcome for a midmorning break or afternoon *café*. Almost from the beginning, Jacques Torres Chocolate was an example of "If you build it, they will come." Not only did we quickly develop loyal customers who were willing to travel some distance to experience our chocolates, but we were also fortunate to have many of America's great chefs order our chocolates to serve in their restaurants. Our tiny shop expanded quicker than we, even in our optimism, had imagined.

From the start, I was determined that we would make only the best. Not only did we search out the world's premium chocolate, but we also made all of our own fillings. Peanut and other nut butters, cream and fruit fillings, and liqueur flavors were all whipped up in our kitchen from the finest ingredients available to us. Even our Champagne truffles were made from Taittinger Champagne, rather than the usual commercial champagne flavor.

As we went into our first winter, we had so many customers waiting on line in the cold that I created a rich, warming hot chocolate drink to keep them happy as they stood in the chilly air. Then we added a few pastries to fulfill requests, but it was the chocolate bonbons and molded holiday figures that established our fame.

We loved our Brooklyn shop, both for the friends we made there and the signal it gave that we were doing the right thing. But the demand for chocolate grew too fast for us to meet it in our small space, so we began looking for a location in Manhattan where could expand our manufacturing capabilities and welcome more new friends. The Brooklyn shop would remain our home base, but we wanted enough room to receive and roast raw cacao beans and to enlarge our research projects focused on creating more signature chocolates. I also wanted to begin developing chocolate bars that we could produce in volume and sell all over the world. I dream big!

In 2004, we opened Jacques Torres Chocolate in Manhattan, again in an area that, unbelievably, hadn't yet been developed to within an inch of its ability to absorb commerce and people. Near the entrance to the Holland Tunnel, which connects New York to New Jersey, we found a street-level space with a truck entrance for receiving cacao beans and shipping chocolates easily, plenty of room to manufacture, and the possibility to grow as expansion became necessary. Again, shortly after we opened, the neighborhood began to take on a new look, with restaurants opening and once-commercial buildings being turned into living spaces.

Our Manhattan-based location, Jacques Torres Chocolate, is a product of my imagination, mixed with a bit of *Charlie and the Chocolate Factory* and a touch of Dr. Seuss. It has a chocolate bar where customers can sip a hot or cold chocolate drink (depending on the season) and eat a pastry or a piece of chocolate. The shopping area has square leather hassocks resembling chocolate blocks placed around small tables, for sitting and relaxing between bites. A large metal sculpture resembling molten chocolate flowing through the air hangs along the ceiling. The display cases hold the bonbons and pastries, while shelves around the shop are stocked with molded chocolate pieces (geared to the season or a specific holiday), bars, specialty chocolate items, and T-shirts, caps, aprons, and other signature merchandise.

We continue to make our filled bonbons in Brooklyn, while most of the molded chocolates and all of the bars and coated ingredients, such as our chocolate-covered cereals, are made in Manhattan. We continue to open new stores throughout the city and, who knows, perhaps in other parts of the country, too. Our online business thrives, and the shops help fill the orders that come through it and the telephone. For me, working with chocolate still translates

to fun. The recipes in this book come from my wish to include it in my life in as many ways as possible. Some of them come from my career as a pastry chef—in France and in America—and some from my exploration of traditional American desserts. And others have come from friends who love to introduce me to their favorite chocolate goodies. Although I now work almost exclusively as a chocolatier, I still enjoy working in the pastry kitchen, so we always feature some chocolate-based desserts in all of our stores. I hope that you will find as much enjoyment in working with chocolate as I have. It is just so marvelous to be able to work with something that is not only delicious, but also good for you!

Types of Chocolate

Throughout most of Europe, dark, intensely flavored bittersweet chocolate reigns supreme, and it was the only chocolate I had worked with before I came to the States. (The Swiss, who embrace the buttery, high-fat, and satin-smooth chocolate for which they are famous, are the exception to this European preference.) When I arrived here, I learned that Americans liked a light, sweet milk chocolate, so I began to incorporate it into my desserts. But as the years have passed, the American palate has changed, and today there is an increase in the demand for more intensely flavored dark chocolate over sweet milk chocolate.

The formulation of a fine-quality chocolate has been a complex and very personal journey for me. I wanted the chocolate that I created to express a distinct flavor that would showcase my own palate, as well as please the palate of the American consumer. In other words,

my chocolate had to appeal across the board. After much experimentation and refinement, I have been able to identify the chocolate that meets both my expectations and the expectations of my customers, and produce it in a number of different types.

First, here is a guide to the various types of chocolate:

Unsweetened: 100% pure cocoa paste (also called chocolate liquor), usually about 53% cocoa butter and 47% cocoa solids, with no sugar added.

Bittersweet: Consists of 35% cocoa paste and 27% cocoa butter, with less than 50% sugar added.

Semisweet: Consists of 27% cocoa butter and 15% cocoa paste, with more than 50% sugar added.

Milk: 40% to 45% chocolate, with the addition of milk solids, sugar, vanilla, and lecithin.

White: Includes no chocolate liquor; made from cocoa butter, milk powder, sugar, vanilla, and lecithin. Compound white chocolates made with the addition of fats other than cocoa butter are of minor quality.

Cocoa powder is made by grinding the "cake" that remains after cocoa butter has been extracted from chocolate. When cocoa powder has been treated with potassium carbonate, an alkaline solution, it is referred to as Dutch processed. The potassium carbonate raises the pH level of the chocolate, which darkens the color and results in a milder flavor. It also makes the cocoa powder easier to dissolve. Untreated cocoa powder, usually called natural unsweetened cocoa powder, has a slightly bitter, acidic taste. I always use Dutch-processed cocoa powder in my recipes. Do not confuse cocoa powder with cocoa mix, which contains sugar and is for making drinks.

Cocoa butter is the pale, almost-cream-colored fat extracted from cacao beans during chocolate making. It is a complex fat, which is one of the reasons that working with melted chocolate can be difficult. I use it as the base for colored decoration of molded chocolates.

We manufacture a few different types of chocolate. Our unsweetened chocolate, made from 100% cocoa solids, is called Ebony. We make two bittersweet chocolates, Dangerously Dark, at 72% cocoa solids, and Jacques' House Blend, at 60% cocoa solids, along with both milk chocolate and white chocolate. In addition, we make special batches, based on the origin of the bean, that vary from 60% to 85% cocoa solids.

Tempering Chocolate

When chocolate is melted, the molecules of fat break up and separate. To reunite them so that you have a workable mix, you must stabilize the chocolate through a heating and cooling process that is known as tempering. This is the most basic skill to master if you want to work successfully with chocolate that you plan to use for candies or pastry decoration. In fact, chocolate will not work its magic unless it is properly tempered.

Tempering, which requires more patience and care than skill, can be done in a variety of ways, but the end result must always be the same: a smooth, pure chocolate that will retain its satiny texture and shiny color once it has set. It can be done three different ways: 1) the demanding traditional, time-consuming (and messy) French way, called *tabliering* whereby two-thirds of the full amount of melted chocolate is poured out onto a cool surface and worked with a spatula until it reaches 81°F and then worked back into the remaining melted chocolate until the whole mass is of a uniform temperature; 2) simply by working with the chocolate over a hot water bath; or 3) in a microwave oven. Since the chocolate must reach and maintain an exact temperature in each case, you need a perfectly calibrated thermometer. I rely on a digital laser thermometer, which is a good investment if you want to make tempering an easy job.

The solid chocolate begins at an average room temperature of 75°F (23°C). Through the melting process, the temperature is raised to between 110° and 120°F (43° and 49°C). It must then immediately be lowered to 82° to 83°F (28° to 29°C) by adding room-temperature chocolate. The added chocolate must be finely chopped, or it will take too long to incorporate it into the melted chocolate and the temperature will go below the necessary 83°F (29°C). It is important that you check the temperature continually; this is not an exact science, as so many factors play into the process. Finally, the liquid chocolate is reheated to the final 88° to 90°F. (White chocolate and milk chocolate will generally melt at 2°F lower than other chocolates because of the amount of lactose they contain.) Meeting and holding these melting, cooling, and warming temperatures are vital to successful tempering.

To temper chocolate in a microwave, put chopped room-temperature chocolate in a microwave-safe bowl, preferably glass, and melt on high for 20 seconds. This should yield a slightly lumpy mix with about one-third of the chocolate still relatively solid. Remove the bowl from the microwave and, using a rubber spatula, transfer the chocolate to a clean, cold bowl. Using a handheld immersion blender, beat the chocolate until it reaches 90°F (32°C) on a thermometer. This is an easy process, but it does take practiced guessing to estimate the initial two-thirds to one-third melting ratio.

You can also temper chocolate by adding small chocolate pieces, called *calets* or *pistoles*, to melted chocolate. They are basically chocolate chips formed into slightly rounded disks. We sell them at Jacques Torres Chocolate for general use (even snacking), and many chocolate manufacturers sell them for use in commercial kitchens. How many pieces you need to add depends on both the temperature of the melted chocolate and the size of the pieces.

You should always temper more chocolate than you think you need, as there is nothing more frustrating than being caught short in the middle of making something. Plus, a larger batch of tempered chocolate will hold its temperature longer. I often use a simple home hair dryer to ensure that the chocolate remains at the correct temperature by blowing the hot air directly over the tempered chocolate. You can also melt a bit more chocolate and add the hot, melted chocolate to the tempered chocolate to raise the temperature. I compare it to ordering an espresso that must be drunk quickly, as the small amount in the cup cools down fast, while a large cup of cappuccino remains hot as you slowly sip it. Plus, tempered chocolate can always be reused. Just pour it into a clean baking pan and seal it tightly with plastic film. When you are ready to use the chocolate, cut it into pieces and treat as though it is a fresh batch of chocolate to be tempered.

If you are simply melting chocolate, never do it over direct heat. It melts best at a temperature of between 104° and 113°F (40° and 45°C) over indirect heat, such as over a hot-water bath. Microwave ovens also do a good job of melting chocolate. But no matter which method you use, always chop the chocolate into small pieces before you begin.

Molding Chocolate

You cannot mold tempered chocolate successfully in wood or other porous materials. Nor is glass a good choice. When you pour tempered chocolate into a glass mold, it immediately takes on the temperature of the glass, which if it is too hot or too cold will cause the chocolate to go out of temper. Antique metal molds, with interiors that have been damaged through years of use or the passage of time, are best used as wall decorations. Flexible plastic molds are terrific, but in time they begin to show wear and must be replaced. All of this is my way of saying that firm plastic and polycarbonate molds are the best choices for molding chocolate.

Although you might have heard that coating a mold with fat will make removing the finished product easier, do not try it. It will not help unmold the item; it will only make it greasy. Chocolate, like plaster, retracts as it cools, which ensures that once it has set it will easily pull away from a plastic mold. Remember, chocolate reflects the surface against which it has been molded, so if properly done, the set chocolate will be smooth and shiny. However, the chocolate must be tempered—not simply melted—or it won't release.

Before you begin to fill a mold, set up your workspace: Have the tempered chocolate in a bowl. Alongside the chocolate have the mold; a ladle; a paring knife, pastry scraper, large metal offset spatula, or other smooth-edged utensil; a wire rack on a parchment- or waxed paper-lined baking sheet; and some clean kitchen towels.

Using the ladle, carefully fill the mold with the liquid chocolate. Once the mold is full, invert it over the bowl of tempered chocolate and allow the excess chocolate to drip back into the bowl. If the mold is finely detailed, it will be necessary to tap on the sides to release any air bubbles that might form in the raised detail. The mold should now be evenly coated with a thin layer (usually ⅛ or 1/16 inch thick, depending on the recipe) of chocolate. Wipe the edge of the mold, or the edge surrounding each cup in the mold, clean with a paring knife or pastry scraper. Place the chocolate-coated mold, open side down, on the wire rack. Let stand for about 5 minutes, or until the chocolate begins to harden. Using the paring knife, scrape the edge of the mold absolutely clean of hardened chocolate. This is important, because the chocolate retracts from the sides of the mold as it sets, and a clean edge will keep it from sticking and cracking as it shrinks. If desired, you can place the mold in the refrigerator for a few minutes to speed the hardening, but do not leave it there for any length of time.

Once you have invested in molds, they can be used over and over again. My best advice for extending the life of plastic or polycarbonate molds is to clean them with care. Wash them in hot, soapy water, carefully wiping them clean with a soft cloth (never any rough material or a scouring pad). Then rinse them well under running water and dry thoroughly, as water deposits can be as damaging to molds as scratchy scrubbers.

Decorating with Chocolate

Decoration brings life to molded figures, brightness to bonbons, and excitement to finished desserts. It is one of my favorite chocolate activities. Décor might be as simple as a few chocolate curls on top of a cake or as elaborate as a molded, painted chocolate centerpiece. Here are seven techniques that I employ to add interest to candies and desserts.

Painting: You can add flair to molded figures with just a few brushstrokes. In general, the area to be painted in a mold is small, so you don't need to mix a large amount of "paint." I recommend using a yogurt maker (the type that has a few small containers) to mix and hold the paints. The temperature of the machine is perfect to keep the paint warm enough to remain constantly spreadable. It is a great place to store cocoa butter paint, too. (Of course, you can also use small stainless-steel bowls over hot water, but the yogurt maker makes the job much easier.) For each color, place a few tablespoons of cocoa butter in a yogurt container. Mix in powdered food coloring, a tiny bit at a time, until the desired color is reached. Then, using a fine-tipped paintbrush, carefully apply the paint to the interior area of the mold you are coloring (for example, red might be used to paint on the mouth of a human or animal figure). Allow the paint to set for about 30 minutes before you proceed with the recipe.

Transfer sheets: These sheets printed with designs are easy to use. Place a sheet, printed side up, on a flat work surface. Using an offset spatula, spread tempered chocolate over the design to cover completely, leaving a smooth, thin layer of chocolate against the transfer sheet. If the chocolate is not smooth, the design will be muddled. As the liquid chocolate hardens, the design will transfer to it. Depending upon the design, the chocolate will take about 10 minutes to set. When it has hardened, carefully peel the transfer sheet from the chocolate. It should come away easily. The sheets can be used with all types of chocolate, but the colors in the design must be bright enough to display on darker chocolate.

Acetate design: Place the chosen design on a clean, flat work surface. Cover with a sheet of acetate. Mix the amount of cocoa butter paint you will need (see Painting, at left). Using a fine-tipped paintbrush and a dark paint, trace the outline of the design on the acetate. Then, use whatever other colors you like to fill in the design. This is rather like a child's paint-by-number kit! Allow the design to dry completely before removing it from the acetate.

Decorative base: Often a molded chocolate piece will need a base. To make one, lay a sheet of acetate on a clean, flat work surface. Using an offset spatula, spread a ¼-inch-thick layer of tempered chocolate over the acetate, taking care to make the base large enough to hold your figure or design. If you want to trim the edges of the base, let the chocolate set for 4 to 5 minutes, or until firm enough to cut but not completely hard, and then trim with a hot (held in or under very hot water for a couple of minutes) sharp paring knife. When the chocolate has set, peel off the acetate.

Marbling: Drizzle enough tempered dark and white chocolate onto a sheet of parchment paper to create a piece of chocolate in the size you require, remembering that the marbled chocolate may be cut into any shape you want. Dip your clean, dry fingertips into the bowl of tempered dark chocolate and begin moving them through the drizzled chocolates to make a marble effect. You will want a layer thick enough to hold its shape once it has hardened, which means it must be at least ⅛ inch thick. Allow to set for 4 to 5

minutes, or until firm enough to cut but not completely hard. Cut with a hot knife as directed for a decorative base, above, or use the tip of an x-acto knife. When the chocolate has hardened, lift off and discard the parchment paper.

Gluing chocolate: The glue that holds molded chocolate pieces together is simply more chocolate! Depending on the number of pieces you are gluing, melt just enough chocolate to make a fine "glue" line between all of the pieces. Place the hardened pieces of chocolate that you want to stick together in the refrigerator for about 15 minutes, so they will be cold enough to "set" the chocolate "glue" immediately when you attach them to one another. Using the melted chocolate just as you would regular glue, and working with two pieces at a time, coat the edge of one piece to be glued with the chocolate and then quickly put the two pieces together and hold them firmly in place. If the hardened chocolate is cold enough, the melted chocolate will set immediately.

Decorating with a cornet: Prepare a cornet by cutting an 8-by-12-by-14½-inch triangle from a sheet of parchment paper. Hold the middle of the long side of the triangle between two fingers of one hand. Take the tip of the triangle on the short, side end and roll it toward the other tip of that same end while simultaneously pulling it in an upward motion. The top of a cone will form where your thumb and finger hold it on the long side. Release your grip from the long side so you are now holding the two corners where they meet. The paper will already resemble a partially formed cone. Then, just roll the remaining tail until it is completely rolled into a cone. There will be one point sticking up from the open end. Fold it inside toward the center and crease the fold. You will now have a cornet. When you fold a filled corner to close it, fold it away from the seam; this will keep the seam from opening. Use a pair of scissors or a sharp paring knife to cut an opening of the desired size at the tip of the cornet and fill the cornet with about ¼ cup tempered chocolate. (You can also use the cornet for piping royal icing, buttercream, or any other firm icing.) Begin piping the chocolate

onto the surface, making swags, dots, or any fine-lined design you like. Or, trace a pattern for, say, flowers or birds in dark chocolate and then fill the outline with milk chocolate or white chocolate.

Piping fine decoration takes practice to achieve neat results. Draw a design on a piece of parchment paper with a felt-tip marker. Repeat the design a few times so you will have more than one example to practice on. Tape the paper in place to keep it from moving while you work. Turn the paper upside down (don't worry, the design is easily seen through the transparent parchment) so that the inked side is on the bottom, which will prevent the toxicity of the ink from affecting the chocolate. Fill the cornet with tempered chocolate and begin tracing the pattern in chocolate. When you feel you have had enough practice, you can immediately begin decorating your dessert. These test runs are not wasteful, as the chocolate can be scraped up and reused.

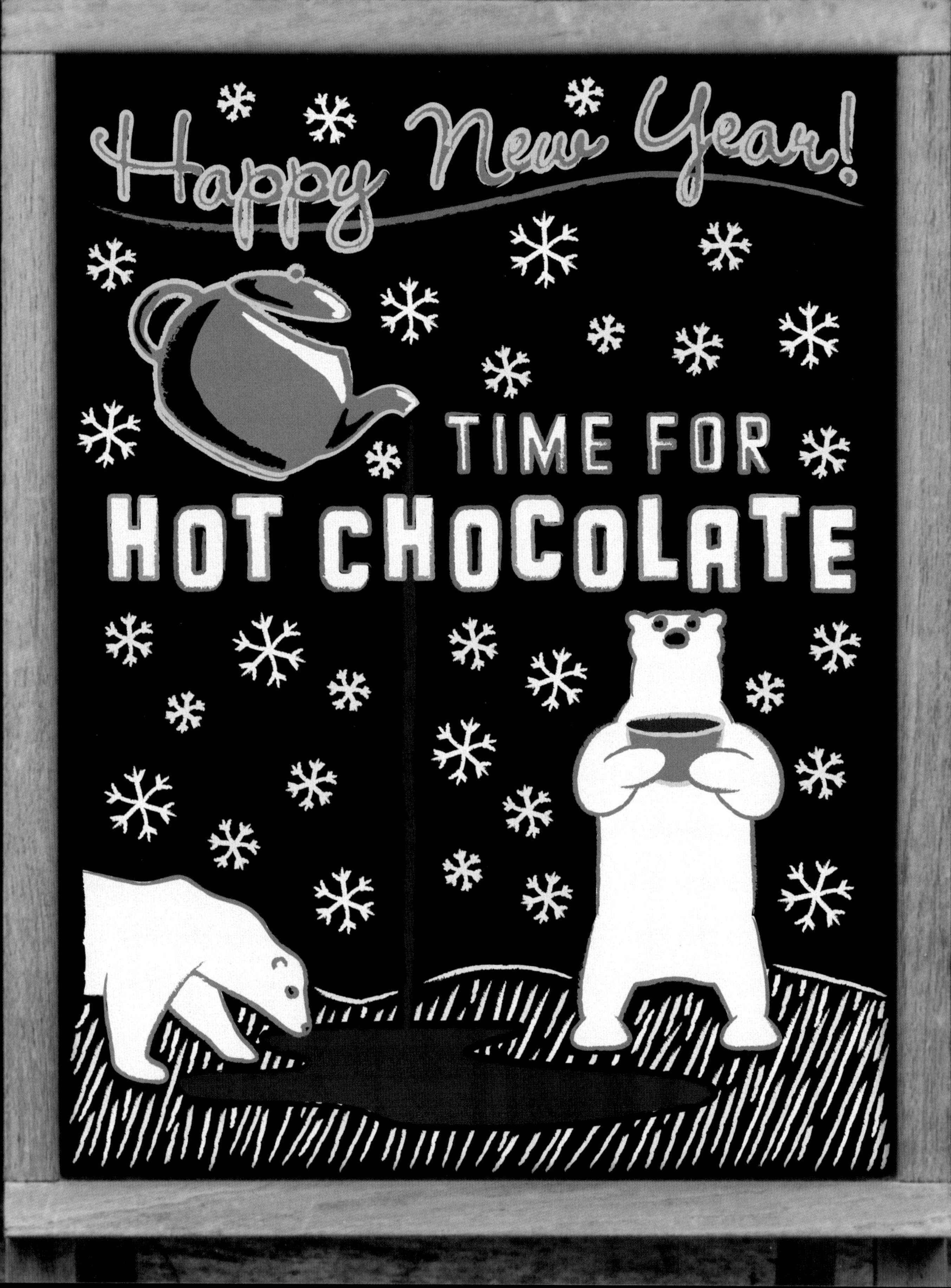
Happy New Year!
TIME FOR
HOT CHOCOLATE

JANUARY

A New Year's Resolution: Let's Eat More Chocolate

January is quiet after the chaos of the busy winter holiday season. The only holiday we have to look forward to during this cold, blustery month is Chinese New Year, and some years, when the lunar calendar takes it into February, we don't even get that. When it does occur, we have a couple of treats up our sleeves for celebrants.

Of course, we all welcome a moment or two to put our feet up and enjoy a cup of steaming hot chocolate, but we also inevitably miss the hectic days of the past few months. However, the quiet only lasts a bit, as we begin planning our schedule for the months ahead. Cacao beans have to be chosen; new equipment investigated; molds, packaging, and gift items ordered; and new recipes devised. The whole staff joins in the process of planning a year at Jacques Torres Chocolate.

Personally, I can think of no better way to begin the year than by making a resolution to eat more chocolate. Not that I need any encouragement, but now that I know that chocolate can be good for me, I have no regrets as I indulge in my passion. Since it is dark chocolate that brings good health tidings, it is fortunate that I prefer the 72% bittersweet chocolate *pistoles* we make in the factory. And should you decide to join me in this resolution, you will have to forsake all other types of chocolate to reap the health benefits. Just remember that an ounce of 72% chocolate daily is good for you!

When I began working with chocolate, I knew that it was wonderfully delicious, but I had no idea that this extraordinary ingredient would also be good for me. Just in the last few years, science has discovered that there are many healthy advantages that accompany eating dark chocolate. In fact, in a 2005 issue of the *Journal of the American Heart Association*, medical researchers reported that eating a 3 ½-ounce bar of dark chocolate daily may help lower high blood pressure in adults suffering from hypertension. Of course, if you consume chocolate high in sugar and additives, the health benefits disappear.

In addition to all of the newly discovered health advantages, chocolate has historically been thought of as one of life's most sensual foods. So, what better way to start the year than with chocolate promoting warm and tender feelings about life and love? Just place a small piece on your tongue and let it elicit good feelings for the months ahead. You'll think only pleasurable thoughts as the silky, smooth melt begins.

Poached Pears
with Chocolate Fondue

Serves 6

This dessert is a great way to start off the year. It's just a bit indulgent, while offering the health benefit of dark chocolate and fresh fruit. You will always find some type of poached fruit on a French dessert buffet, and for this recipe I simply expanded a classic French dish. I pair Bosc pears, which are firm enough to hold their shape when cooked, with a luscious fondue to accent their simple goodness.

If I were going to serve poached pears *sans chocolat*, I would use wine as the poaching liquid. However, since these pears are filled with a pear liqueur–flavored chocolate fondue, they don't require the additional deep flavor of wine. If you are feeding kids or don't like alcohol, eliminate the liqueur from the fondue. The pears will still be delicious.

1 lemon, cut in half crosswise

6 ripe Bosc pears with stems intact

6 cups water

1 cup sugar

Pear-Flavored Chocolate Fondue (recipe follows)

Fill a bowl large enough to hold the pears with water. Add the juice from half of the lemon. As you peel and core each pear, slip it into this acidulated water to keep it from discoloring.

Select a deep, lidded saucepan large enough to hold the pears for poaching. Cut a piece of parchment paper into a circle slightly smaller than the diameter of the pan. This will be used to cover the fruit and keep it immersed in the poaching liquid as it cooks. Set aside.

Peel the pears, leaving the stem intact. Using a small, sharp knife, carefully core each pear from the flower end, leaving the pear whole. This will allow the poaching liquid to flow into the interior of the pear, cooking and flavoring it evenly. Cut a very thin slice from the flower end so that the pears can stand upright. Put the pear in the acidulated water and repeat with the remaining pears.

Pour 6 cups fresh water into the saucepan. Add the sugar and the juice from the remaining lemon half, place over medium-high heat, and bring to a simmer, stirring to dissolve the sugar. Add the pears, cover with the parchment-paper circle followed by a lid, adjust the heat as needed to maintain a gentle simmer, and cook for about 10 minutes. Begin checking for doneness by inserting a long toothpick (or the very point of a small, sharp knife, as you don't want to affect the appearance of the pear) into a pear. It should offer just a tiny bit of resistance when pierced. This may take anywhere from 10 to 25 minutes.

Remove the pears from the heat and, if serving immediately, use a slotted spoon to transfer them, cored end down, to a wire rack placed in a baking pan to catch the draining liquid. (If not using immediately, carefully transfer the pears, along with the poaching liquid, to a clean container. Let cool, cover, and refrigerate for up to 3 days. When ready to use, drain well and proceed with the recipe.)

When the pears are very well drained—almost dry—neatly cut about 1 inch off of the stem end of each one. Pat dry with a paper towel. You should now have a bottom half that forms a cup with a top lid.

If making a buffet platter, cover the bottom of a large serving plate with fondue. If making individual servings, spoon a generous amount of the fondue into the center of each of six dessert plates. For the buffet platter, place all of the pear bottoms in the fondue. For individual servings, place a pear bottom in the center of each dessert plate. Carefully spoon the fondue into the "cup" of each pear. Place the top "hat" on the side or slightly off to the edge on the top of each pear. Serve immediately.

Pear-Flavored Chocolate Fondue

10 ½ ounces bittersweet chocolate, chopped

1 ¼ cups heavy cream

2 tablespoons pear eau-de-vie such as Poire William

Place the chocolate in a heatproof bowl. Set aside.

Place the cream in a small, heavy-bottomed saucepan over medium heat and heat just until distinct bubbles begin to form around the edges of the pan. Remove from the heat and slowly pour about half of the hot cream over the chocolate. Let stand for 30 seconds, until the chocolate begins to melt, and then begin stirring with a wooden spoon.

As the mixture starts to smooth out, add the remaining cream and stir gently to blend well. Add the liqueur and stir to incorporate. Set aside until ready to use. If made in advance, when ready to serve reheat the fondue in the top half of a double boiler set over simmering water.

Chocolate-Covered Fortune Cookies

Makes 3 dozen

Everyone in New York celebrates Chinese New Year. Chinatown is ablaze with fireworks and dragon parades, and neighborhood restaurants have special New Year's menus. We all become Chinese for just one evening.

These little treats are easy to make and add a bit of finesse to the everyday end of a Chinese take-out meal. If you are having a big party or celebrating a special event that will require hundreds of fortune cookies, many manufacturers will insert special sayings for an additional charge. You will then have to spend a couple of days dipping to make them complete. It is helpful to have long needle-nosed tweezers for holding the cookies as you dip.

36 crisp fortune cookies

——

12 ounces bittersweet chocolate, tempered (page 13)

——

Line a rimmed baking sheet with parchment paper. Place a wire rack on top of the parchment. Line the fortune cookies up in a single layer on a work surface.

Pour the chocolate into a warmed bowl. Using long needle-nosed tweezers, grasp a cookie, carefully dip it into the chocolate, lift it out, and allow the excess chocolate to drip back into the bowl. Carefully lay the coated cookie, one of the fairly flat open sides down, on the wire rack. Repeat to coat all of the cookies. Let stand for about 15 minutes, until the chocolate sets.

If not serving the cookies immediately, store in a single layer in an airtight container at room temperature for a day or two. Do not try to keep them any longer, as they will absorb moisture and turn flabby.

Chocolate Blackout Cake
with Ganache Drizzle

Makes 4 small cakes

This is a very simple yet spectacular dessert. You can add decorations (page 16) that will take it over the top, or, if it is a lazy day, you can eliminate the chocolate décor and just drizzle some ganache on the plate and sprinkle a few fresh berries over it. You could also bake one big cake, but it won't make the same dramatic statement these little towers do.

To make this cake, you will need four sets of standard round metal dry-measure measuring cups, with 1-cup, ½-cup, ⅓-cup, and ¼-cup measures in each set. Few home cooks have that many sets, so rather than buy them—unless, of course, this becomes a family favorite—I suggest that you borrow them from your neighbors. The only problem is that you will probably have to share your baking bounty with them.

6 tablespoons unsalted butter, cut into pieces, at room temperature

——

¼ cup very hot, strong brewed coffee or 2 tablespoons coffee extract

——

¾ cup buttermilk

——

2 large eggs, at room temperature

——

1 cup plus 2 tablespoons sugar

——

1⅔ cups cake flour

——

⅓ cup Dutch-processed cocoa powder

——

1 teaspoon baking powder

——

½ teaspoon baking soda

——

Pinch of salt

——

1 teaspoon pure vanilla extract

——

Ganache Drizzle (recipe follows)

——

One solid piece of block white chocolate, for garnish, optional

Preheat the oven to 350°F. Line a rimmed baking sheet with parchment paper. Place a wire rack on top of the parchment paper. This will be used for cooling and icing the cakes.

Line a second rimmed baking sheet with parchment paper. Set aside.

Lightly coat the interior of each cup of four sets of measuring cups with nonstick baking spray. Set aside.

Combine the butter and coffee, stirring to melt the butter. When melted, whisk in the buttermilk. Set aside.

Combine the egg and sugar in the bowl of a stand mixer fitted with the paddle attachment. Beat on low speed to just combine. Add the flour followed by the cocoa powder, baking powder, baking soda, and salt, one ingredient at a time, and continue beating on low, mixing to just combine. Add the vanilla and finally blend in the coffee mixture.

Using a glass measuring cup (simply for ease of pouring), fill each measuring cup about half-full with the batter. Place the filled cups on the parchment-lined baking sheet and put in the oven. Bake for 15 to 20 minutes, or until the center of each cake is set, noting that the smaller cakes will bake quicker than the larger ones.

Remove the cakes from the oven, then carefully invert them onto the wire racks. When cool, set the cakes into four stacks on the wire racks, placing the largest cake on the bottom and working up to the smallest. Using an offset spatula, spread the Ganache Drizzle over the cakes, allowing the excess to drip down the sides onto the baking pan. Using a clean spatula, carefully transfer each cake to a dessert plate.

If decorating with white chocolate, pull a vegetable peeler over the block of white chocolate to create chocolate "curls" directly onto each cake.

Ganache Drizzle

7 ounces bittersweet chocolate, chopped

——

⅔ cup heavy cream

——

Place the chocolate in a heatproof bowl. Set aside.

Place the cream in a small, heavy-bottomed saucepan over medium heat and bring to a bare simmer. Do not allow it to boil or it will bubble over the pan.

Remove from the heat and slowly pour about half of the hot cream over the chocolate. Let stand for 30 seconds until the chocolate begins to melt. Then, using a wooden spoon, begin beating the mixture. As it starts to smooth out, add the remaining cream and continue to beat until the mixture is very smooth and glossy. If you add all of the cream at once, the heat hitting the cold chocolate will cause the fat in the chocolate to separate out and the ganache will not firm up. (If desired, you can use an immersion blender to ensure a very smooth ganache.)

Let stand at room temperature until the cakes are ready to ice. If the ganache firms up too much before spreading, place it in the top half of a double boiler over simmering water and, using a wooden spoon, stir to soften, then proceed with the recipe.

Chocolate Chess Pie

Makes one 9-inch pie

I created this version of the old-fashioned American chess pie, which I learned how to make from my friend and co-author Judie Choate. It was the signature dessert pie at her bakery, and she convinced me that it was the ultimate chocolate sensation. I still don't know why it is called chess pie, although I've been told that it comes from a baker who, when asked what was in the oven that smelled so good, responded, "jes' ["just" in southern vernacular] pie." The taste of this pie is rich and smooth. If you like, serve it with a dollop of unsweetened whipped cream. I use a classic French pastry for the crust, but you can use your own favorite recipe or, in a pinch, a store-bought frozen pie crust.

Pâte Brisée (recipe follows)

1 cup sugar

½ cup Dutch-processed cocoa powder

1 tablespoon all-purpose flour

3 large egg yolks

1 large egg

3 tablespoons water

2 teaspoons white vinegar

½ cup (1 stick) unsalted butter, melted and cooled to room temperature

Make the pastry dough and line the pan as directed. Preheat the oven to 350°F.

Combine the sugar, cocoa powder, and flour in a mixing bowl. Set aside.

In the bowl of a stand mixer fitted with the paddle attachment, combine the egg yolks, whole egg, water, and vinegar. Beat on medium speed until frothy. Slowly add the butter, beating until incorporated. Then slowly add the sugar mixture, beating until thoroughly blended.

Pour the batter into the prepared pastry shell. Bake for about 35 minutes, or until the pastry is golden and the center is set. Transfer to a wire rack and let cool for at least 15 minutes before cutting into wedges to serve.

Pâte Brisée

Makes one 9-inch pie or tart crust

1 ⅔ cups cake flour

———

Pinch of salt

———

Pinch of sugar

———

½ cup (1 stick) plus 2 tablespoons chilled, unsalted butter, cut into small cubes

———

Scant ⅓ cup ice water

———

In a bowl, combine the flour, salt, and sugar. Add the butter and toss to coat evenly with the flour. Using your hands, work the butter into the flour until the mixture resembles coarse meal. Try to do this quickly, because if your hands get too warm the butter will melt and the dough will be tough. Add the water and, still using your hands, quickly work the water into the flour mixture just until the dough comes together. Do not overmix, or the dough will become tough.

Pat the dough into a disk shape and wrap it in plastic film. Place in the refrigerator for about 30 minutes to relax the gluten before rolling out.

When ready to roll, remove the dough from the refrigerator and place it on a lightly floured surface. Lightly flour a rolling pin and roll the dough out to an 11-inch circle about ¼ inch thick. Roll the circle around the rolling pin and carefully transfer the dough to a 9-inch pie or tart pan. Gently press the dough into the pan, fitting it onto the bottom and against the sides.

If using a pie pan, turn the excess pastry around the edge under and against the rim of the pan and press gently to make a neat edge. Starting at the edge opposite you, pinch dough between your thumb and index finger around the edge of the pan at ½-inch intervals to form a fluted design all around. Keep turning the pie as you work.

If using a tart pan, remove the excess dough around the edge by gently pushing the rolling pin over the top of the pan to make a nice clean edge.

With either pan, dock the bottom of the pastry by randomly poking it with a kitchen fork. Refrigerate until you are ready to use.

For this particular recipe, the pastry shell is used unbaked. However, for recipes requiring a baked pie shell, it can be baked in a preheated 375°F oven for about 25 minutes.

Chocolate-Covered Almond Clusters

Makes about 5 dozen clusters

Sweet, crunchy, and wonderfully delicious, these confections are a cinch to make. Keep some on hand for instant gratification or last-minute gift-giving any time of the year. Although I use almonds, you could use almost any toasted nut pieces, or even pumpkin seeds.

4 cups slivered blanched almonds, toasted

12 ounces milk chocolate or white chocolate, tempered (page 13)

Line a rimmed baking sheet with parchment paper. Set aside.

Place the almonds in a large bowl. Add half of the chocolate and, using a rubber spatula, toss to coat the nuts evenly with the chocolate. The chocolate will immediately begin to set. Once it has firmed completely, add the remaining chocolate, tossing to coat the nuts evenly a second time.

Using a tablespoon, quickly form the chocolate-coated almonds into small mounds on the prepared baking sheet. Try to work very quickly, as the chocolate will harden quite fast, particularly if your kitchen is cool. (If the kitchen is warm, transfer the candies to the refrigerator for a few minutes to harden.) Let stand until the chocolate has set.

Serve immediately, or layer the almond clusters in an airtight container, separating the layers with waxed paper, and store at room temperature for up to 2 weeks.

Jacques's Famous Orange Hot Chocolate Mix

Serves 4

This is the key to my kingdom. Sipping a cup of this steaming hot chocolate has turned many of my customers into loyal fans. It makes a great homemade treat to keep on hand all year long—for easy entertaining or to keep on hand for house gifts. For the latter, place enough to make 4 servings in an attractive tin and label with instructions (see below). You can easily double, triple, or quadruple this recipe. Three tips to keep in mind: grate the chocolate on the smallest holes of a box grater, don't boil the water or milk before adding the chocolate mix, and whisk as you go to create a nice frothy top.

1 ½ cups (about 8 ¼ ounces) finely grated bittersweet chocolate

―――

½ cup dry whole-milk powder

―――

Freshly grated zest of 1 orange

―――

Pinch of freshly ground cinnamon

―――

In a bowl, combine the chocolate, milk powder, orange zest, and cinnamon and whisk to distribute the ingredients evenly. Use immediately, or store in an airtight container at room temperature for up to 2 weeks.

To make 1 serving of hot chocolate: Combine ½ cup hot chocolate mix with 1 cup very hot water (or milk) in a small, heavy-bottomed saucepan over medium heat. Bring to a boil while whisking constantly. Remove from the heat and pour into a cup. Garnish with marshmallows (store-bought or homemade, page 182), if desired, and serve piping hot.

To make 1 serving of spicy hot chocolate: Proceed as directed for the hot chocolate, but add ground cayenne pepper to taste to the hot chocolate mix. I don't recommend adding more than ½ teaspoon cayenne per ½ cup of the mix, unless you like to eat fire. When serving, I like to put a cinnamon stick in the cup, as it adds a deeper flavor to the chocolate-chile combo.

Chocolate-Ginger Cookies

Makes 3 dozen cookies

This is a perfect cookie to serve with tea in celebration of the Chinese New Year or to simply add some warmth on a cold, wintry day. The spicy ginger resonates through the chocolate with Asian tones.

The cookie dough is quite easy to make and forgiving. I sometimes use a special flexible baking sheet with 1- to 1½-inch dome-shaped cavities (available from Sur la Table) to make these cookies, and they can also be formed in a cookie press. But simplest of all is the slice-and-bake method, which results in spicy little disks. If you're feeling inspired, or need a slightly fancier dessert, add to these cookies the flourish of chocolate fans.

Six 1-inch pieces candied ginger

———

4 large egg yolks, at room temperature

———

1 cup confectioners' sugar

———

¾ cup (1½ sticks) cold unsalted butter, cut into small pieces

———

½ vanilla bean

———

1½ cups all-purpose flour

———

½ cup Dutch-processed cocoa powder

———

Pinch of baking powder

———

Pinch of salt

———

Chocolate Fans (recipe follows), optional

———

Preheat the oven to 400°F.

Line two baking sheets with silicon mats or parchment paper. Set aside.

Place the candied ginger on a large piece of plastic film, then cover it with another piece of film. This is to keep the rolling pin from sticking to the ginger. Using a rolling pin, press back and forth on the ginger to mash it into a paste.

Combine the mashed ginger with the egg yolks, confectioners' sugar, and butter in the bowl of a standing electric mixer fitted with the paddle.

Cut the vanilla bean in half lengthwise and, using the blade of a small, sharp knife, scrape the seeds from the bean into the bowl with the other ingredients.

Turn the motor on low and mix the dough for about 1 minute, or until well blended.

Combine the flour, cocoa powder, baking powder, and salt and add the dry mixture to the butter mixture. Continue beating on low until just combined. Do not overmix or the dough will become tough.

Scrape the dough from the bowl and place it on a clean, flat work surface. Using your hands, roll the dough back and forth to form it into a rope that is about 1½ inches in diameter. If the dough is sticky, lightly flour your hands. Using a small, sharp knife, cut the dough rope, crosswise, into ¼-inch-thick pieces.

Place the dough slices on the prepared baking sheets. Transfer to the preheated oven and bake for about 20 minutes, or until set and lightly browned around the edges.

Remove the cookies from the oven and transfer to wire racks to cool. If desired, decorate each cookie with a Chocolate Fan.

Chocolate Fans

8 ounces bittersweet or white chocolate, tempered (page 13)

Using an offset spatula, carefully spread a thin layer of tempered chocolate out on a cool, flat work surface—marble is best. Using the spatula, carefully clean around the edges so that you have a neat rectangle. Allow the chocolate to set slightly— just long enough for it to be pliable, yet still hold its shape.

Place one hand on the handle of a cake triangle or small bench scraper and rest your thumb on its blade. Push the triangle through the chocolate to make strips about 2 inches wide and 3 inches long. Use your thumb to catch one side of the chocolate to push it into a pleated shape, thereby creating a small chocolate fan. Pinch the short side to pull the chocolate together to form a tight handle for the fan. Let rest for about 30 minutes to harden completely before using.

FEBRUARY

Mardi Gras, Valentine's Day, and Chinese New Year

It's a good thing that January is a bit quiet, because February roars in, bringing us one of our busiest times of the year. It is interesting to try to understand how chocolate came to be associated with Valentine's Day and, throughout the year, with romance. In its very early years, chocolate was thought to be an evil potion and its consumption was quite restricted. The Aztecs, however, considered it an aphrodisiac, and their emperor, Montezuma, reportedly drank a chocolate mixture daily to increase his virility. Many observers assume that it is his endorsement that led to chocolate going hand-in-hand with love. Today, scientific findings that link eating dark chocolate with an improvement in mood (through its boost of the brain chemical serotonin) only reinforces its role as an elixir for affairs of the heart.

We have learned about many Valentine's Day traditions from our customers. But for me, one of the most unusual came to our attention through our many Japanese customers. On Valentine's Day in Japan, only women give the gifts, almost always chocolate, though other tokens of respect are also offered. The chocolate gift is one of two types: obligatory (*giri choco*) or romantically intended (*honmei choco*).

Obligatory chocolates are just as their name implies, gifts to bosses, coworkers, friends, or other men to whom a token of respect can be presented without any romantic meaning attached to it. These are usually small, inexpensive chocolates and, depending on her status, a single woman may distribute tens of these. *Honmei choco*, on the other hand, is generally an expensive box of bonbons that may also be accompanied by another substantial gift to indicate that the recipient is indeed someone special. (So women are recipients as well, Japan also celebrates White Day, on March 14, when men return a gift of chocolate, always packaged in white wrapping, to the women who have honored them on Valentine's Day.)

*Strawberry Tuxedo Gents
and Gowned Ladies*

———

Chocolate Bonbons

———

Valentine Sweethearts

———

Chocolate Indulgence

———

*Chocolate-Coated
Dried Cherries*

———

Chocolate Soufflé

———

Lots of Hot Chocolate Drinks

———

An interesting chocolate statistic in the United States is that while women purchase about 75 percent of all chocolate bought during the year, an equal percentage is purchased by men in the days leading up to Valentine's Day—most commonly at the last minute. In fact, at the store, we can readily identify the look of the romantically challenged gentleman as he rushes through the door only minutes before closing time, credit card in his grasp, sweat on his brow, and fear in his eyes that we might be sold out of the chocolate he knows he has to have in hand. We've developed a reputation for catering to these customers. Our staff immediately arranges to have the gift wrapped with a card attached, and the customer's panic subsides.

Of all of the chocolates we carry, two of them tie for all-time favorite Valentine's Day gift: Strawberry Tuxedo Gents and Gowned Ladies and Body Butter, a secret concoction we make in the shop. The strawberries are delicately dressed for romance in white and dark chocolate.

Strawberry Tuxedo Gents and Gowned Ladies

Makes 2 dozen strawberries

These strawberries are not nearly as difficult to make as you might think. All you need are perfect strawberries, tempered dark and white chocolates, and a steady hand. I find it easier to work with a parchment-paper cornet than with a pastry bag, as you can cut the tiniest hole in the tip for drawing the fine lines and dots of chocolate. The amount of chocolate will be more than enough for two dozen berries, so you can make a few extra, if you like, as cook's treats. I can't imagine them going to waste!

24 large, perfect organic strawberries, stems attached (see note)

———

8 ounces bittersweet chocolate, tempered (page 13)

———

8 ounces white chocolate, tempered (page 13)

———

Line a rimmed baking sheet with parchment paper. Make 2 parchment-paper cornets (page 18), and cut a tiny opening in each tip.

One at a time, pat the berries dry with a paper towel to ensure that absolutely no moisture is clinging to them.

Place the tempered bittersweet chocolate in a warmed bowl and the white chocolate in another warmed bowl. Working with one berry at a time and holding it by its stem, carefully dip one side, on the diagonal and almost to cover completely, into the dark chocolate. You need to leave a small area near the stem uncoated. Carefully place on the parchment paper, and let stand for about 5 minutes, or until set (see photograph).

When all of the berries have been dipped in the dark chocolate and the chocolate has set, begin dipping the opposite side of each berry into the white chocolate. Again, place the berries on the parchment paper and allow the chocolate to set completely (see photograph).

When the chocolate has set, fill 1 cornet with dark chocolate and the other with white chocolate. Without touching the berries, paint a tiny bow tie directly on the exposed fruit on 12 of the berries. Then, pipe a row of tiny "studs" down the front of the 12 berries, positioning them directly below the bow tie (see photograph). Now, decorate the remaining 12 berries. Again, without touching the berries, paint a "ruffle" of white chocolate around the edge of the "bodice" of the "chocolate dress," and then pipe a tiny necklace around the "neck" of the exposed fruit (see photograph).

Allow the chocolate to dry fully before serving. These do not keep more than a few hours.

NOTE: I use organic strawberries so that I don't have to wash them. The surface of a strawberry readily absorbs moisture, which makes it difficult for the chocolate to cling to it.

Chocolate Bonbons

Makes about 5 dozen bonbons

There is nothing more romantic than a box of chocolate bonbons. Surprisingly, as elegant and delicate as chocolate bonbons appear, they are really quite easy to make. You do have to have molds (firm plastic ones are inexpensive and durable) tempered chocolate (page 13), and a bit of time. But if you enjoy working with chocolate, they can be fun to make and experiment with. The molds come in a wide variety of sizes and can be of a very simple design, for traditional round bonbons, or they may be quite elaborate.

I am constantly trying new flavor combinations to create enticing candies. We make many different fillings, flavored with Champagne, passion fruit, or chiles, for example, that only heighten the romance. We create all of our fillings from scratch, whether using homemade peanut butter or exotic fruits and nuts. The fillings included here are just two of the many that we make every day, and either one will make enough to fill at least 5 dozen bonbons. Both flavors are a splendid match with bittersweet chocolate.

2 pounds chocolate, preferably bittersweet, tempered (page 13)

―――

½ recipe Raspberry Ganache (recipe follows)

―――

½ recipe Passion Fruit Ganache (recipe follows)

―――

Line a rimmed baking sheet with parchment paper. Place 1 or 2 wire racks large enough to hold the candy molds on the baking sheet. Set aside.

Place the tempered chocolate in a warmed stainless-steel bowl. Following the directions for molding chocolate on page 15, carefully ladle the chocolate into the molds. Turn the molds upside down over the bowl of tempered chocolate, allowing the excess chocolate to drip out, leaving just a thin coating (about ¹⁄₁₆ inch) on each indented cup. Wipe the edge of the mold on the rim of the bowl to clean off the edge. Tap the edge of each mold to release any air bubbles that might remain in the chocolate, to ensure a perfectly smooth coating, then place each chocolate-coated mold, open side down, on the wire rack. Let stand for about 5 minutes to allow the chocolate to begin to set.

Just before the chocolate has fully set (*recrystallized* is the technical term), use a paring knife or pastry scraper to clean the excess chocolate from the molds, returning it to the tempered chocolate. Set the molds cavity side up on a clean work surface.

Spoon the Raspberry Ganache into a pastry bag fitted with a ¼-inch plain tip. Carefully fill half of the chocolate cups with the soft ganache, stopping within about ¹⁄₁₆ inch of the rim. Repeat with the Passion Fruit Ganache and the remaining chocolate cups. Place the filled molds on the wire rack on the baking sheet. Place the pan in the refrigerator for about 5 minutes to allow the chocolate to set completely. If the chocolate has been properly tempered, you should be able to see a faint air space between the chocolate and the molds when the chocolate has set.

Remove the molds from the refrigerator and lightly cover the top with plastic film. Set aside to rest in an air-conditioned environment for at least 8 hours or up to overnight to set completely. This step is very important, because if the ganache is not firm, it will weep into the chocolate when the final coating is put on.

When the ganache is set, melt the remaining tempered chocolate again and carefully ladle the chocolate over the filled molds, covering the filling with a thin layer and scraping off the excess chocolate with a paring knife or pastry scraper. When you finish, each filled cup should be sealed with chocolate and the surrounding mold should be completely clean. Set aside to firm for about 30 minutes.

Line a large rimmed baking sheet with parchment paper. When the bonbons are firm, release them onto the parchment by flipping the mold upside down, bending it slightly, and tapping it on the side.

Put on thin latex or vinyl gloves, such as those worn by medical professionals. This will keep the bonbons fingerprint-free as you move them. If desired, place each bonbon in its own paper cup. Arrange the bonbons in a single layer in an airtight container and store in a cool or air-conditioned environment (under 72°F) for up to a week.

Raspberry Ganache

Makes about 4 cups

1 ⅓ cups pure raspberry purée
(see note)

⅓ cup light corn syrup

¼ cup heavy cream

13 ounces milk chocolate,
finely chopped

3 ounces bittersweet chocolate,
finely chopped

4 tablespoons unsalted butter,
cut into small pieces, at room
temperature

3 tablespoons raspberry eau-de-vie

In a heavy-bottomed nonreactive saucepan, combine the raspberry purée, corn syrup, and cream. Bring to a boil over low heat. Immediately remove from the heat and, using a whisk, beat to lower the temperature slightly.

Add the milk chocolate and bittersweet chocolate and let stand for 4 minutes. Then whisk the chocolate into the raspberry mixture to incorporate. Using an immersion blender, beat the mixture until cooled to just barely under 130°F on an instant-read thermometer.

Add the butter and eau-de-vie and, using the immersion blender, mix until the ganache registers 110°F. If necessary, place over a pan of hot water to keep slightly warm until ready to use. Just be sure that the bottom of the bowl (or pan) holding the ganache does not touch the hot water or it will cause the ganache to get too warm and soft.

NOTE: Raspberry purée is available at specialty stores or online (see Sources, page 192).

Passion Fruit Ganache

Makes about 4 cups

1 cup passion fruit purée (see notes)

⅓ cup heavy cream

2 tablespoons light corn syrup

1 ¼ pounds milk chocolate, chopped

4 tablespoons unsalted butter, cut into pieces, at room temperature

¼ cup Alizé passion fruit liqueur (see notes)

NOTES:

Passion fruit purée is available at specialty food stores or online (see Sources, page 192).

Alizé, a French company, makes a variety of liqueurs, including Gold Passion, a passion fruit liqueur made with Cognac. Alizé liqueurs are carried in most well-stocked liquor stores.

In a heavy-bottomed nonreactive saucepan, combine the passion fruit purée, cream, and corn syrup. Bring to a boil over low heat. Immediately remove from the heat and, using a whisk, beat to lower the temperature slightly.

Add the chocolate and let stand for 4 minutes. Then whisk the chocolate into the passion fruit mixture to incorporate. Using an immersion blender, beat the mixture until cooled to just barely under 130°F on an instant-read thermometer.

Add the butter and liqueur and, using the immersion blender, mix until the ganache registers 110°F. If necessary, place over a pan of hot water to keep slightly warm until ready to use. Just be sure that the bottom of the bowl (or pan) holding the ganache does not touch the hot water or it will cause the ganache to get too warm and soft.

Valentine Sweethearts

Serves 6

Crisp cookie hearts sandwiching two creamy flavors of mousse, this sensational romantic dessert will win the heart of any suitor. It is easy on the cook because the mousse and cookies can be made in advance and the dessert can be put together at the last minute. I love the addition of the chocolate decorations, but you don't need them to enjoy this heartfelt dessert.

If you don't have two pastry bags, make two parchment-paper cornets (page 18) and cut off the tip of each to make a ⅜-inch opening.

2 cups Bittersweet Chocolate Mousse (page 82)

2 cups White Chocolate Mousse (page 82)

6 Chocolate-Covered Sugar Cookie Hearts (recipe follows)

Chocolate Décor (recipe follows)

Outfit 2 pastry bags with large plain tips. Fill one bag with the dark mousse and the other with the white mousse.

Line a baking sheet with parchment paper, and place the cookie hearts on the parchment. Working with 1 cookie at a time, carefully pipe dark chocolate mousse onto one-half of each heart, covering it completely. Then, pipe the white mousse onto the other half, again covering it completely and taking care that each color remains separate.

Place a chocolate décor on each heart and serve.

Chocolate-Covered Sugar Cookie Hearts

Makes ten 2½-inch heart-shaped cookies, with extras

¾ cup (1½ sticks) plus 2 tablespoons unsalted butter, cubed, chilled

——

¾ cup plus 2 tablespoons confectioners' sugar

——

½ cup almond flour

——

2 large eggs, at room temperature

——

1 vanilla bean, split in half lengthwise

——

1 cup pastry flour

——

1 cup all-purpose flour

——

Pinch of salt

——

1 pound bittersweet chocolate, tempered (page 13)

——

Combine the butter, confectioners' sugar, and almond flour in the bowl of a stand mixer fitted with the paddle and mix on low. Then add the eggs and beat on medium speed for about 2 minutes, or until the mixture resembles scrambled eggs.

Using the edge of a small, sharp knife, scrape the seeds from the vanilla bean into the butter mixture. Add the pastry flour, all-purpose flour, and salt and beat on medium speed for about 1 minute, or until well blended. Do not overwork the dough, or it will be tough.

Scrape the dough from the bowl onto a clean work surface and pat it into a rectangle. Wrap in plastic film and refrigerate for at least 30 minutes or up to overnight. Preheat the oven to 350°F. Line 2 cookie sheets with parchment paper.

Lightly flour a clean, flat work surface, and place the dough in the center. Using a rolling pin, roll out the dough into a rectangle about ⅛ inch thick. If the dough sticks to the pin or the surface, lightly dust either one (or both) with flour. Using a 2½-inch-wide heart-shaped cookie cutter, cut out 10 hearts. You will only need 6 cutouts, but the extras will allow for breakage (and eating). Using an offset spatula, transfer the hearts to the prepared baking sheets, spacing them about 1 inch apart. (You will have more dough than you need for this recipe. Cut it into any shapes you like and bake them along with the hearts.)

Bake for about 10 minutes, or until light brown around the edges. Remove from the oven, immediately transfer the cookies to wire racks, and let cool completely.

Line the baking sheets with clean parchment paper. When the cookies are cool, set aside 6 cookies to use for the dessert. The remaining cookies can be stored in an airtight container at room temperature for up to 1 week. Carefully dip one side of each cookie into the tempered chocolate, and place the cookies, chocolate side up, on the prepared pans. Let stand for about 15 minutes to allow the chocolate to set.

When the chocolate has set, dip the other side of each cookie in the tempered chocolate and return the cookies, wet chocolate side up, to the pans. Let stand for about 30 minutes to allow the chocolate to harden thoroughly.

Chocolate Décor

8 ounces bittersweet chocolate,
tempered (page 13)

———

8 ounces white chocolate,
tempered (page 13)

———

Place 2 sheets of parchment paper on a clean, flat work surface. Make 2 parchment-paper cornets (page 18) and cut off the tip of each to make $\frac{1}{16}$-inch opening. Fill 1 cornet with dark chocolate, and fill the other cornet with white chocolate.

Working with one cornet at a time, gently push on the cornet, simultaneously pulling up and out to make a slight arc of chocolate that is thick at the bottom and comes to a flowing point at the top. Repeat this motion, attaching each new arc to the previous one at the bottom, until you have 6 to 8 delicate arcs. You will need one of each type of chocolate for each dessert. Let the chocolate harden for about 30 minutes before carefully removing the decorations from the paper and setting them on the desserts.

Chocolate Indulgence

Makes 4

There was a time when almost every pastry chef had his or her own secret recipe for a "molten" chocolate cake—and with good reason. This is an almost-perfect dessert: easy to make, deliciously inviting with a crusty exterior and a runny center, and always delectable. The cakes are particularly kind on the home cook, as the batter can be made up to 24 hours in advance and the ramekins filled, covered with plastic film, and refrigerated until ready to bake. It is important to bake them until the exterior is just set and the center is still a bit shaky, so the chocolate oozes when the cake is cut.

6 ounces bittersweet chocolate, finely chopped

6 tablespoons unsalted butter, at room temperature

¼ cup sugar

2 large eggs, at room temperature

1 tablespoon all-purpose flour

About ½ cup Chocolate Sauce (page 186), warmed

1 cup raspberries

Preheat the oven to 400°F. Have ready four ½-cup ramekins, muffin molds, or disposable aluminum cups. If they are not nonstick, lightly coat them with nonstick baking spray. Arrange the ramekins on a rimmed baking sheet.

In the top half of a double boiler, combine the chocolate, butter, and sugar. Place over (not touching) barely simmering water in the bottom pan and heat, stirring constantly with a wooden spoon, until melted, fully blended, and smooth. Add the eggs one at a time, whisking well after each addition. Remove from the heat and add the flour, stirring just to combine.

Divide the batter evenly among the ramekins, and place the baking sheet in the oven. Bake for 12 minutes, or until just set, slightly cracked on top, and gooey in the interior. Do not overbake, or the cakes will be too firm. Remove from the oven and let stand for about 5 minutes.

Pool about 2 tablespoons of the warm sauce in the center of each dessert plate. Invert a ramekin over each pool of sauce, tapping it gently with your fingers to unmold the warm cake. Sprinkle each plate with an equal amount of the raspberries and serve immediately.

Chocolate-Coated Dried Cherries

Makes 2 pounds

The flavor pairing of sweet-tart cherries and rich, dark chocolate is just delectable and a perennial favorite. These confections are easy to make and wonderful to have on hand for a snack, dessert, or gift giving. I like mine to be thickly coated with chocolate, but if you prefer a light coating, just use less chocolate. The optional coating of confectioners' sugar or cocoa powder takes these little gems to the stars!

3 ½ cups dried pitted sweet cherries

1 ¼ pounds bittersweet chocolate, tempered (page 13)

1 ¾ cups confectioners' sugar or Dutch-processed cocoa powder, optional

Line a large baking sheet with parchment paper.

Place the cherries in a large bowl. Add about 1 cup of the chocolate and, using a rubber spatula, immediately begin folding the cherries and chocolate together. Keep folding until the cherries are lightly but thoroughly coated. Then continue gradually adding chocolate and folding it over the cherries until you have used all of the chocolate and the cherries are thickly coated. As you fold, try to separate any cherries that cluster or clump together.

If you are not using confectioners' sugar or cocoa powder, transfer the cherries to the prepared baking sheet, spreading them out in a single layer, and let stand until the chocolate has completely set. If you are using the confectioners' sugar or cocoa powder, leave the chocolate-coated cherries in the bowl until the chocolate is just firm and then add the sugar or cocoa and toss to coat well. You can also transfer half of the cherries to a second bowl, and coat half of them with ¾ cup plus 2 tablespoons confectioners' sugar and the other half with the same amount of cocoa powder. Transfer the cherries to the baking sheet and let stand until the chocolate has completely set.

Layer the cherries, separated by sheets of parchment paper, in an airtight container and store at room temperature for up to 2 weeks.

Chocolate Soufflé

Serves 6 to 8

There is nothing that says celebration like a chocolate soufflé. Not only does a towering soufflé, fresh out of the oven, look sensational, but it is also one terrific low-fat dessert. Plus, this particular recipe is perfect for entertaining as the batter can be made up to one day in advance, held in the refrigerator, and baked while you enjoy your meal.

Soufflés can also be made and baked in buttered and sugared individual soufflé molds. This is best done by piping the soufflé batter into the molds with a pastry bag fitted with a 1-inch plain tip. Fill as directed in the recipe and bake for 6 to 8 minutes.

Approximately 1 tablespoon softened unsalted butter

¾ cup granulated sugar

---

8 large egg whites, at room temperature

3½ ounces bittersweet (preferably 75%) chocolate, melted

---

2 tablespoons confectioners' sugar

Whipped cream, optional

Preheat the oven to 375°F.

Lightly coat the interior of a 1½-quart soufflé mold with the butter. Place ¼ cup of the granulated sugar in the mold and begin turning the mold back and forth so that the entire interior is generously coated with sugar. Turn upside down to allow any excess sugar to fall out. Set aside.

Combine the egg whites with the remaining ½ cup granulated sugar in the bowl of a standing electric mixer, whisking to combine.

Fill a 1-quart saucepan halfway with water and place it over high heat. Bring to a boil. Place the bowl over the boiling water without allowing the bottom of the bowl to directly touch the water. Using a wire whisk, beat for about 3 minutes, or until quite warm.

Remove from the heat and place the bowl in the stand mixer fitted with the whip attachment. Beat on medium just until frothy. Increase the speed to medium-high and beat until stiff but not dry peaks form.

Remove the bowl from the mixer and, using a rubber spatula, fold the melted chocolate into the meringue, taking care not to overmix, but also taking care that the egg whites are completely incorporated into the chocolate.

Carefully scrape the soufflé batter into the prepared mold. It should come to about 1 inch below the top. Place in the middle of the oven, making sure that it has room to rise without hitting a top rack. Bake for about 20 minutes, or until the soufflé has risen to about one and a half times its height and the top is lightly colored.

Remove from the oven. Place the confectioners' sugar in a fine-mesh sieve and, tapping on the sides of the sieve, dust the top of the soufflé with the sugar. Serve immediately with a bit of whipped cream, if desired.

Lots of Hot Chocolate Drinks

Makes 1 cup

Is there anything more delicious on a cold winter day than a cup of steaming hot chocolate? Rather than just a plain cup, here are a few variations to warm your heart and soul.

You can vary the intensity of the chocolate by adding more or less chopped chocolate to the hot milk. As a variation on the traditional marshmallow garnish, I love topping hot chocolate with a big scoop of whipped cream and shavings of bittersweet chocolate.

1 cup whole milk

——

2 ounces bittersweet chocolate, chopped

——

Suggested Flavorings

1 vanilla bean, cut in half horizontally and then split lengthwise, or ½ teaspoon pure vanilla extract OR

——

1 peppermint candy cane OR

——

1 teaspoon freeze-dried coffee granules, dissolved in 1 tablespoon hot water OR

——

5 raspberries OR

——

Pinch each of ground allspice, ground cinnamon, ancho chile powder, and chipotle chile powder

——

In a small, heavy-bottomed saucepan, heat the milk over medium heat. When it is slightly warm, gradually add the chocolate while whisking constantly. Cook, whisking constantly, until the milk begins to form bubbles around the edge of the pan. Do not allow the milk to boil.

For vanilla: Using the edge of a small, sharp knife, scrape the seeds from the vanilla bean into the milk, then add the bean to the pan. Whisk in the chocolate. Remove the vanilla bean before serving. Or, if using the extract, simply add it to the hot chocolate.

For peppermint: Stir the milk with the candy cane, allowing it to melt partially into the mixture as it heats.

For coffee: Add the diluted coffee with the chocolate.

For raspberry: Using a wooden spoon, crush the raspberries into the milk after the chocolate has melted.

For spices: Add the allspice, cinnamon, and chiles to the hot milk before you add the chocolate. Add the chiles to taste, keeping in mind that freshly ground chile can be very hot.

VARIATION:

Hot White Chocolate: Use ½ cup each whole milk and heavy cream in place of the milk; 3 ½ ounces white chocolate, chopped, in place of the bittersweet chocolate; and ½ teaspoon pure vanilla extract for the flavoring. Prepare as directed.

MARCH & APRIL

Saint Patrick's Day, Easter, and Passover

Spring is my favorite time of the year. I love the birth of trees, leaves, and flowers—everything a brilliant new green. Easter and Passover are the celebrations that reign during this season, although we do get our share of St. Patrick's celebrants. At Jacques Torres Chocolate, the Easter holiday means chocolate bunnies, chocolate eggs, chocolate chickens, and scores of other chocolate figures. We have chocolate cowboy bunnies, chocolate bunnies on tractors, chocolate bunnies in race cars, and multicolored chocolate roosters crowing. It's all about fun.

Passover means chocolate matzo in six different varieties. Chocolate-covered apricots, chocolate-covered ginger, and whatever other fun treats we can bring to the celebration are also on the shelves. Everything is tied in cellophane with bright ribbon and a sprig of flowers. Chocolate craziness runs the show!

My mentor, Louis Franchain, arrives from France in the weeks prior to Easter and we are often joined by Sottha Khunn, with whom I worked at Le Cirque. Since so much of what we do this time of year is handwork, there can never be too many hands in the chocolate, as the genesis of thousands and thousands of chocolate bunnies, chicks, lambs, and eggs occurs. Plus, because the Passover season usually arrives at the same time as Easter, we also need hands to design treats incorporating matzo. (We don't have a kosher kitchen, so we don't have a full line of Passover desserts.)

Much of the preparation for the final week before Easter, one of the busiest weeks in our year, has occurred months in advance. Working with the staff and based on previous sales, we have decided which of the traditional molds will be used; estimated how many of each style will be produced; ordered baskets, ribbons, and trim; hired temporary workers; and focused our attention on creating new products to entice both the press and our loyal customers into the stores.

Molded Chocolate Bunny

Chocolate-Covered Matzo

Mudslides

Chocolate Marshmallow Eggs

Peanut Butter Chocolate Eggs

Chocolate Sticky Pudding

Chocolate-Banana Roll

Chocolate Ladyfingers

At the factory, Easter has become about the fantasy of beautifully decorated chocolate figurines in sizes ranging from small enough to hold in a toddler's hand to so big that it can barely be held in the arms of a sturdy ten-year-old. We are fortunate to live in a multicultural city, so we make sure that, no matter what religious beliefs are followed, we have a chocolate treat to suit everyone's celebration.

For me, the Easter season is invigorating. I love every minute I spend painting and filling the animal molds. The production kitchen is overwhelmed with tray upon tray stacked with the smaller chocolate figures, while the shelves are filled with larger-than-life-sized bunnies and nesting hens. When the spirit moves us, giant hollow eggs are molded, filled with smaller goodies, and then festively decorated: some with three-dimensional chocolate forms, some with traditional floral trim, and some with a combination of both. The store is brimming with baskets and with children anxious to have the Easter bunny deliver them safe and sound to their bedsides on Easter morning. Our chocolate figures seem to serve no other purpose than to make children smile, and even after a long day pouring chocolate, they still make me smile too.

Molded Chocolate Bunny

One 12-inch bunny

To create a successful molded figure, you must use tempered chocolate to ensure a smooth, snappy finish. Making the mold is rather like working with plaster except that chocolate is far messier! Antique metal molds are absolutely beautiful but not terribly effective, as the hardened chocolate will stick to the metal mold and crumble as you try to remove it. The best types of molds are plastic or polycarbonate. As they are the most reliable, I work with modern plastic molds and I strongly recommend that you do also. Just remember that the temperature of your kitchen will affect the speed at which the chocolate sets.

Plastic molds usually come in two equal parts, which must be united before filling with chocolate. I suggest that you clip the two parts together using small steel binder clips (available from all office supply stores). You can tape the parts together with heatproof tape, but the clips are much more efficient.

If this is your first attempt at making a molded figure, I suggest that you make a simple chocolate bunny without the painted trim.

4 ounces cocoa butter (optional)

———

Food coloring powder (optional)

———

2 pounds bittersweet chocolate, tempered (page 13)

———

If you are going to paint the bunny's face and other elements, decide on the colors you are going to use and then divide the cocoa butter into the number of colors selected. Place the cocoa butter in a yogurt maker (page 17) or individual stainless-steel bowls, using enough cocoa butter to keep it liquid, work the coloring powder into each one, and then, using a small paint brush, carefully paint the features directly onto the interior of the mold as directed on page 17. Allow the cocoa butter to set for about 30 minutes, then proceed with the recipe. If you don't have the time or energy to make the cocoa butter colors, simply paint the face with tempered milk or white chocolate.

Place a wire rack on a baking sheet lined with parchment paper. Set aside.

Place the tempered chocolate in a warmed bowl.

Clip the two parts of the mold together. Then, holding the mold upside down, pour the tempered chocolate into the mold. When it is full, immediately empty it back into the same bowl. The mold should be evenly coated with anywhere from $1/16$ to $1/8$ inch of chocolate. Tap the edge of the mold to release any air bubbles that might remain in the chocolate, to ensure a perfectly smooth coating. Wipe the edge of the mold clean on the edge of the bowl (you don't want to waste a drop of chocolate) and place the mold, open end down, on the wire rack. Let stand for about 5 minutes, or until the chocolate has begun to set.

Once the chocolate hardens, using a paring knife, scrape the open end of the mold clean. As the chocolate hardens, it will retract from the mold, and the clean edge helps prevent the chocolate from sticking and cracking as its shrinks. (If your kitchen is warm, place the mold in the refrigerator for a couple of minutes to facilitate hardening.)

Repeat this process 2 more times, allowing the chocolate to thoroughly harden between pourings, to give a nice thick, child-friendly coating of chocolate.

Once the chocolate has set, unclip the mold and lift the plastic from the chocolate form. If desired, wrap in cellophane and store in a cool, dry spot for up to 5 days.

Chocolate-Covered Matzo

Makes about 10 ounces

L issa Guttman is the chocolate boss in our company. She runs her part of our business with a huge smile and an iron fist! She is constantly researching new ideas, new packaging, and new policies. In addition to her superb attention to detail, she has been a wonderful teacher to me, educating me about the traditions of the Jewish holidays and helping me identify places where chocolate can play a role in them. She taught me how important matzo is to the Passover gathering, explaining that it has a specific place on the Seder plate and that children traditionally enjoy a hunt for missing matzo during the Passover celebration. I thought that it might make the hunt more interesting if we covered the matzo in chocolate. This was a very good guess, because chocolate-dipped matzo has been a big hit. We now make it in four different varieties: peanut butter, coconut, *mendiant* (studded with nuts and dried fruits), and wickedly spiced. I hope it becomes your favorite take-to-the-Seder gift.

1 pound bittersweet or semisweet chocolate, tempered (page 13)

One 10-ounce box matzo

<small>SUGGESTED TOPPINGS</small>

½ cup chopped pistachios, pecans, macadamia nuts, or walnuts OR

¼ cup whole pistachios, ¼ cup dried cranberries, and 3 tablespoons grated fresh coconut OR

½ cup grated fresh coconut

Line a rimmed baking sheet with parchment paper. Set aside.

Place the chocolate in a warmed bowl. Break the matzo into large pieces, or keep it whole. Using tongs and working with one piece at a time, dip the matzo into the chocolate, immersing only about ½ inch. Lift the matzo up out of the chocolate, allowing the excess to drip off. Keep dipping the piece, ½ inch at a time, until the whole piece is covered. This method keeps the chocolate coating smooth and neat.

Carefully transfer the chocolate-covered matzo to the prepared baking sheet and let stand until set. Continue dipping the matzo pieces until you have as many as you wish.

If you want to add any one of the toppings to one side, sprinkle it on before the chocolate hardens. If you want to add it to both sides, add it to the first side as directed, and allow the chocolate to harden. Then, turn the matzo piece over, brush with chocolate, sprinkle with the topping, and let stand until hardened.

Layer the matzo, separated by sheets of waxed paper, in an airtight container and store at room temperature for up to 5 days.

Mudslides

Makes 20 large cookies

Melted chocolate and chocolate pieces combine to make these the most "chocolatey" cookies possible. Once you've had a Mudslide, I will guarantee that it will be your cookie of choice for Easter baskets, lunch boxes, cookie jars—well, you get it. People tell us that these are their favorite cookies in the world, and that they taste best hot and oozy straight from the oven. Mudslides freeze well and can easily be popped into the microwave to get that same oozy rush.

1 pound 60% bittersweet chocolate, chopped, plus 1 pound 60% bittersweet chocolate, finely chopped

6 ounces unsweetened chocolate, chopped

½ cup plus 3 tablespoons all-purpose flour

2 ¾ teaspoons baking powder

1 ¼ teaspoons salt

5 large eggs, at room temperature

6 tablespoons unsalted butter, at room temperature

2 ¼ cups sugar

1 ¼ cups chopped walnuts

Preheat the oven to 350°F. Line 2 cookie sheets with parchment paper or silicone mats, or use nonstick pans.

Combine the 1 pound chopped bittersweet and the unsweetened chocolate in the top half of a double boiler. Place over (not touching) gently simmering water in the bottom pan and heat, stirring frequently, until completely melted. Remove from the heat and set aside.

In a bowl, stir together the flour, baking powder, and salt and set aside. Crack the eggs into another bowl and set aside.

In the bowl of a stand mixer fitted with the paddle, beat the butter on medium speed until very light and fluffy. Add the sugar and beat until well blended. Add the eggs and beat just until incorporated. Then add the melted chocolate and beat to combine. On low speed, add the flour mixture a little at a time, beating after each addition until incorporated before adding more.

Remove the bowl from the mixer and fold in the finely chopped chocolate and the walnuts with a rubber spatula.

To shape the cookies, scoop out heaping tablespoonfuls of the dough, form them into balls, and place them on the prepared baking sheets, spacing the balls about 1 inch apart. Bake the cookies for about 15 minutes, or until set around the edges. Remove from the oven and transfer the cookies to a wire rack to cool slightly. Serve warm.

Leftover cookies can stored, airtight, at room temperature for 3 days or, tightly wrapped, frozen for up to 1 month.

Chocolate Marshmallow Eggs

Makes about 3 dozen

With a crisp outer shell of chocolate and a gooey mashmallow interior, these eggs are an Easter-basket favorite. If we have any left after Easter, I like to pop one on top of a mug of hot chocolate for a special treat. You can either decorate the eggs with chocolate, or you can simply dip the entire egg in tempered chocolate. If dipping, you will need to temper about 1 pound of chocolate to cover all the eggs. Then, working with 1 egg at a time, place it on a dipping fork, dip the entire egg in the chocolate, and then lift it out, allowing the excess chocolate to drip off. I prefer bittersweet, but milk or white chocolate will also work. You will need plastic or polycarbonate egg molds with each side forming half an egg that, when filled, clip together to make perfectly shaped eggs. They are available at most candy- and cake-supply stores.

¼ cup cornstarch

½ cup plus 1 tablespoon light corn syrup

1 ½ cups sugar

¾ cup water

3 tablespoons unflavored powdered gelatin

2 or 3 drops concentrated natural oil such as peppermint or orange

4 ounces bittersweet chocolate, tempered (page 13)

Spray the interior of the egg molds with nonstick vegetable spray. Place the cornstarch in a fine-mesh sieve and lightly dust the interior of the mold, coating evenly. Tap out the excess cornstarch. Set aside.

Place ¼ cup plus 1 tablespoon of the corn syrup in a heatproof bowl. Set aside.

In a heavy-bottomed saucepan, combine the sugar, the remaining ¼ cup corn syrup, and ½ cup of the water. Clip a thermometer to the side of the pan, and place the pan over medium heat, stirring frequently, until the mixture registers 110°F.

While the sugar mixture is heating, combine the gelatin with the remaining ¼ cup water in the top half of a double boiler. Place over (not touching) boiling water in the bottom pan and heat, stirring occasionally, for a few minutes, or until the gelatin has melted or "bloomed." Do not allow the mixture to boil.

Pour the hot sugar mixture and the bloomed gelatin into the bowl of corn syrup. Using a wire whisk, beat for about 5 minutes, or until fluffy. Beat in the flavored oil.

Spoon an equal portion of the mixture into each of the prepared molds. Clip the molds together so that the two halves will come together to form an egg shape. Set aside for 8 hours or up to overnight, until very firm.

When set, unclip the molds. The whole egg shapes can be easily tapped from the molds.

Fill a pastry bag fitted with a plain fine tip or a cornet (see page 18) with tempered chocolate. Decorate the eggs in any design you wish—a child's name, flowers and leaves, or an Easter bunny are just a few ideas. (Or, working with one at a time, place an egg on a dipping fork and dip the entire egg in chocolate, allowing the excess to drip off.) Place on a parchment paper–lined baking sheet to set until the chocolate hardens completely. The eggs should be eaten within 24 hours.

Peanut Butter Chocolate Eggs

Makes about 2 dozen, depending on mold size

Who doesn't love the combination of chocolate and peanut butter? These eggs are like an upscale version of Reese's Peanut Butter Cups. You can actually make them in any mold you like, but I generally make them egg-shaped. To do it my way, you will need plastic or polycarbonate egg molds (see page 67) to make perfectly shaped ovals. They are available in various sizes at most candy- and cake-supply stores.

Note that you are not making whole egg shapes, but rather an open half that will be filled with the peanut butter mixture. The molds are available at most candy and cake supply stores. Make sure that they are very clean and dry before using, or the chocolate will stick.

10 ½ ounces bittersweet chocolate, tempered (page 13)

———

5 ounces bittersweet chocolate, chopped

———

Generous 2 cups (about 18 ounces) smooth peanut butter

———

Line a rimmed baking sheet with parchment paper and place a wire rack on the parchment. Set aside.

Place the tempered chocolate in a warmed bowl. Following the directions for molding chocolate on page 15, carefully ladle the chocolate into the mold, taking care that the chocolate covers the entire mold. Turn the mold upside down over the bowl of tempered chocolate, allowing the excess chocolate to drip out, leaving just a thin coating on each indented cup. Tap the edge of the mold to release any air bubbles that might remain in the chocolate, to ensure a perfectly smooth coating. Wipe the edge of the mold clean on the edge of the bowl (you don't want to waste a drop of chocolate), then place the chocolate-coated mold, open side down, on the wire rack. A bit more chocolate will drip off. Let stand for about 4 minutes to allow the chocolate to begin to set.

Just before the chocolate has fully set, use a paring knife or pastry scraper to clean the excess chocolate from the edge of the mold, returning it to the tempered chocolate, so that the finished eggs will have nice clean edges and to make it easier to unmold them.

Transfer the mold, cavity side up, to the refrigerator. Let rest for 10 minutes to allow the chocolate to harden and retract from the sides of the mold.

Line the baking sheet with a clean piece of parchment paper. Remove the mold from the refrigerator and invert it onto your hand. The egg shells should fall out. If not, rest your thumbs on the outside edge of the mold and place your first two fingers on the inside of the chocolate egg shape. Gently begin to lift the chocolate from the mold. Do not press or pull too hard or the chocolate will break. Carefully place the egg shapes on the prepared baking sheet until they are ready to be filled.

To make the filling, place the chopped chocolate in the top half of a double boiler. Place over (not touching) gently simmering water in the bottom pan and heat, stirring frequently, until completely melted. Remove from the heat and set aside until just cool to the touch. Do not allow it to get too cold or it will begin to harden.

While the chocolate is cooling, place the peanut butter in the bowl of a stand mixer fitted with the paddle and beat on medium speed just until softened. Add the slightly warm chocolate and beat until combined. The mixture will be quite stiff, so make sure it is well blended.

Using a teaspoon, fill each egg shape with the peanut butter mixture, smoothing the top with a spatula or knife. If you prefer a soft filling, let the eggs rest at room temperature for about 1 hour before serving. If a firmer texture is preferred, place the eggs in the refrigerator for about 15 minutes to allow the filling to harden, then serve.

Store, in a single layer, covered and refrigerated, for up to 3 days.

Chocolate Sticky Pudding

Serves 6

This is a terrific old-fashioned American dessert. I use homemade marshmallows here, but you can also use the commercial variety to speed the preparation. The pudding is best served warm from the oven.

If you want to serve individual portions, prepare the sugar syrup and then divide it evenly among six 2-cup soufflé-type dishes. Place 2 marshmallows in the bottom of each dish and then spoon an equal portion of the batter on top.

1 cup all-purpose flour

⅓ cup Dutch-processed cocoa powder

1 teaspoon baking powder

2 tablespoons unsalted butter

½ cup granulated sugar

½ cup milk

1 teaspoon pure vanilla extract

¾ cup toasted walnuts or pecans

1½ cups water

½ cup dark brown sugar

12 Chocolate Marshmallows (page 182) or large store-bought marshmallows

Whipped cream or Vanilla Ice Cream (page 122) for serving, optional

Preheat the oven to 350°F. In a bowl, sift together the flour, cocoa powder, and baking powder. Set aside. Have ready a 1½-quart casserole dish.

In the bowl of a stand mixer fitted with the paddle, combine the butter and granulated sugar and beat on low speed just to combine. Raise the speed to medium-high and beat until well incorporated. Begin adding the flour mixture alternately with the milk, beating to combine Add the vanilla and beat to incorporate. Remove the bowl from the mixer and, using a rubber spatula, fold in the nuts until evenly incorporated. Set aside.

In a heavy-bottomed saucepan, combine the water and brown sugar. Place over medium heat and bring to a boil, stirring to dissolve the sugar. Lower the heat to a simmer and cook for 5 minutes. Remove from the heat and pour into the casserole dish. Place the marshmallows on top of the liquid. They should immediately begin to melt.

Drop the chocolate batter by the heaping tablespoonful evenly over the marshmallows. Do not stir.

Bake for about 45 minutes, or until the sauce has bubbled up through the cake and a cake tester inserted into a solid piece of cake comes out clean. Serve warm with whipped cream or Vanilla Ice Cream, if desired.

Chocolate-Banana Roll

Serves 6

I first made this dessert for a food and wine celebration at Florida's Epcot Center. It was such a success and so easy to put together that I gave it a permanent place in my repertoire. Bananas and chocolate are about as good a pairing as peanut butter and chocolate—everybody seems to love the mix. The only element that has to be made is the almond cream, which will keep for a few days in the refrigerator, making the dessert ideal for easy entertaining. It can be served out-of-hand for a great kid's snack, or it can be fancied up by arranging beautiful bias-cut pieces on a dessert plate with a few dots of chocolate sauce around them.

Almond Cream (recipe follows)

2 sheets frozen phyllo dough, thawed and held according to manufacturer's directions

Approximately 3 tablespoons melted butter

Approximately 3 tablespoons confectioners' sugar

1 ripe, firm banana, peeled and cut, lengthwise, into quarters

Approximately 1 cup bittersweet or semisweet chocolate bits

Approximately ¼ cup Chocolate Sauce (page 186), optional

Preheat the oven to 350°F.

Line a baking sheet with parchment paper. Set aside.

Place the Almond Cream in a pastry bag fitted with a ½-inch round tip. Set aside.

Place a single sheet of phyllo dough on a clean, flat work space with the longest part facing you. Using a pastry brush, lightly coat it with some of the melted butter. Sprinkle with confectioners' sugar. Place the remaining sheet of phyllo on top and repeat the buttering and sugaring.

Lay the banana pieces along the edge closest to you, leaving about a 1½-inch border. Pipe the Almond Cream along both sides of the bananas. Generously place chocolate pieces along the outer edge of the cream.

Starting from the edge closest to you, fold the phyllo over the filling and continue rolling the phyllo over to make a neat, tight roll. Fold firmly and tightly, leaving the seam side down, because if the phyllo is loose, the filling will spill out as it bakes. Brush the top of the roll with melted butter and place on the prepared baking sheet.

Bake for about 25 minutes, or until the phyllo is golden brown and the filling is hot and a bit oozy.

Remove from the oven and allow to rest for about 5 minutes before cutting, on the bias, into equal pieces.

If desired, serve on a pool of Chocolate Sauce or drizzled with Chocolate Sauce.

Almond Cream

½ cup (1 stick) plus 1
tablespoon unsalted butter, at
room temperature

⸻

Generous ½ cup sugar

⸻

Generous 1 cup almond flour

⸻

1 large egg, at room
temperature

⸻

Scant ¼ cup all-purpose flour

⸻

½ tablespoon dark rum

⸻

Combine the butter and sugar in the bowl of a stand mixer fitted with the paddle and beat on medium until well blended. The mixture will be sandy until the butter begins to absorb the sugar. Add the almond flour and continue to beat on medium for about 4 minutes, or until the mixture is light and fluffy. Add the egg and continue beating, scraping down the inside of the bowl from time to time, for about 3 minutes, or until the mixture is light and creamy. It is important to beat long enough for the batter to become light and fluffy as it incorporates air so that the end result will not be dense and heavy.

When the mixture is light and fluffy, add the all-purpose flour and beat for about 1 minute or just long enough to incorporate the flour. Do not overbeat, as the mixture will loose its delicate texture as the gluten in the flour develops. Fold in the rum.

If not using immediately, transfer the mixture to an airtight container and refrigerate until needed, or for up to 5 days. If refrigerated, the mixture will darken and harden somewhat. When ready to use, bring to room temperature and then again beat with an electric mixer to lighten it in texture and color.

Chocolate Ladyfingers

Makes about 4 dozen cookies

E very pastry chef learns how to make these traditional sponge-cake-like cookies early on in their education, and I can tell you they're not easy to make. This version, with cocoa, of course, is much simpler, I guarantee. It is difficult to achieve the light texture that makes these cookies the perfect accompaniment to ice cream or an exquisite base for fruit or ice cream desserts. But the effort is well worth it.

Ladyfingers can be piped into their fingerlike shape directly onto a baking sheet with a pastry bag, or they can be formed in a specially designed ladyfinger pan, which has oblong indentations.

Ladyfingers freeze well, so they are terrific cookies to keep on hand for use in an elaborate dessert like tiramisù or a French charlotte.

¾ cup plus 2 tablespoons cake flour

¼ cup Dutch-processed cocoa powder

8 large egg yolks, at room temperature

6 large egg whites, at room temperature

¾ cup granulated sugar

¼ cup confectioners' sugar

Preheat the oven to 400°F. Line 2 rimmed baking sheets with parchment paper. Set aside.

Sift together the flour and cocoa powder into a bowl. Set aside. In a large bowl, lightly beat the egg yolks until blended. Set aside.

In the bowl of a stand mixer fitted with the whip, beat the egg whites on medium speed for about 2 minutes, or until foamy. Add the granulated sugar a tablespoon at a time. When all of the sugar has been added, increase the speed to medium-high and beat for about 3 minutes, or until the egg whites are slightly stiff. Reduce the speed to low and continue to beat for an additional 2 minutes, or until stiff, but not dry, peaks form. Beating at this lower speed allows the egg whites to absorb more air without drying out. If the egg whites begin to separate or look very dry, stop beating immediately.

Using a rubber spatula, begin gently folding the egg yolks into the whipped whites, folding just until the yolks are partially incorporated. Then, gently fold the flour-cocoa mixture into the egg whites, taking care not to deflate the whites. Be sure to reach all the way to the bottom of the bowl so that the mixture is completely blended.

Spoon the batter into a pastry bag fitted with a ¾-inch plain tip. Pipe ¾-inch-wide finger-length lines of batter onto the prepared baking sheets, spacing them about ½ inch apart. It helps if you hold the pastry bag at a slight angle and allow the tip to just touch the parchment as you start to squeeze. Also, squeeze gently, so you can achieve the length you want without wavering, and then abruptly stop squeezing and lift the tip straight up, leaving a little curly tail at the end of each ladyfinger. When all of the cookies have been formed, place the confectioners' sugar in a small fine-mesh sieve and, tapping the side of the sieve, dust the cookies with the sugar.

Bake for about 5 minutes, or until lightly browned. Watch carefully, as it is difficult to see the browning on the chocolate batter and you don't want them to overbake. Remove from the oven, immediately transfer the cookies to wire racks, and let cool completely.

Place the ladyfingers in layers separated by waxed paper in an airtight container and store at room temperature for up to 2 days or in the freezer for up to 2 weeks.

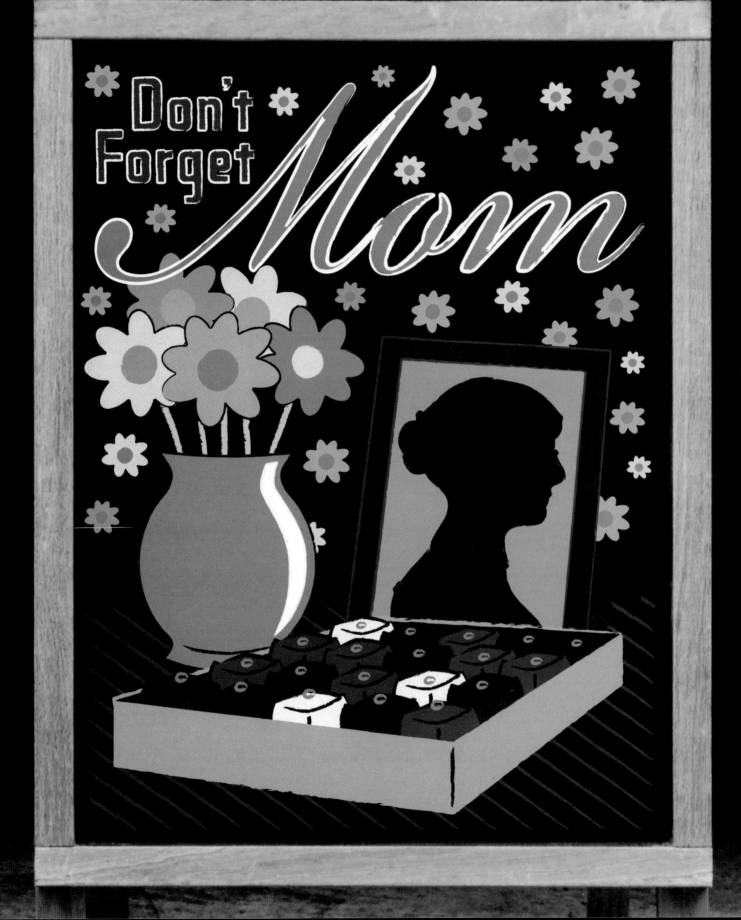

MAY

*Cinco de Mayo, Mother's Day,
and Getting Ready for Summer*

May begins with a great big chocolate bang on the fifth with Cinco de Mayo, the commemoration of Mexico's defeat of the French in the Battle of Puebla in 1862. Even though I am a Frenchman, how could I not celebrate Cinco de Mayo? Mexico plays such an important role in the history of chocolate that the crew at Jacques Torres Chocolate simply has to raise a little ruckus to honor the nation. Although in Mexico, Cinco de Mayo is celebrated mainly in the state of Puebla, it is an enormous holiday in the United States in communities along the border with Mexico and in American cities, like New York, with large Mexican-American populations.

Since the days of the ancient Aztecs and Maya, cacao has been integral to Mexican culture. It was once so esteemed that the beans themselves were used as currency. Today, chocolate still rules throughout Mexico, and having spent considerable time learning from country's artisanal chocolate makers, I have come to appreciate their traditions. I love celebrating Cinco de Mayo in part because it reminds me of the generosity of the Mexican people, the beauty of their country, and the richness of their culture.

In Oaxaca, the center of Mexican chocolate making, many small shops sell chocolate drinks and treats made right before your eyes, restaurants all have an exceptional mole sauce, and every home cook has secret recipes for ceremonial chocolate drinks. In fact, Oaxacans reportedly eat and drink about five times more chocolate than their countrymen.

The traditional methods of working with cacao are still in practice throughout Mexico but are most in evidence in Oaxaca. Beans are ground by hand using a *metate y mano* (a stone slab and rolling pin), and the recipes, typically mixing cacao, spices, sugar, and almonds, have been passed down for generations. Marketplaces are dotted with stalls offering freshly made hot chocolate, a wondrous drink made from water or milk that inspired my own hot chocolate (page 55). Its distinctive frothy top is created by twirling a *molinillo*, a long wooden stirrer, between the palms of your hands. *Champurrado,* another hot drink, is made from *masa harina* (hominy flour), sugar, and chocolate and belongs to the family of thick beverages known *atoles*, which date from the time of the Incas. My appreciation of these Mexican chocolate traditions and many others brings a Cinco de Mayo celebration to our calendar.

Right on the heels of our day of Mexican madness comes Mother's Day. When I was a pastry chef, Mother's Day was one of our busiest days because it is the one day that every mother gets a day off from cooking. And it remains a busy day for me, as boxes of bonbons and bags of specialty chocolate creations are carried or sent to treasured moms.

Through our customers, I have learned that Mother's Day is celebrated in many countries, though not always on the second Sunday in

Savory Chocolate Napoleon

―――

Chocolate Mousse

―――

Chocolate Hot Tamale

―――

Chocolate Angel Food Cake

―――

Fours Pochés

―――

Chocolate Crème Brûlée

―――

Esterel Cake

―――

Chocolate Sticky Buns

May, as it is in the United States. In France, Mother's Day usually falls on the last Sunday in May, except in those years when religious observances push it to the first Sunday in June. I always make sure to create a special treat for my mom.

I have almost as much fun thinking up specialty chocolates for moms for Mother's Day as I do thinking up bunnies for kids at Easter. It is a challenge to dream up chocolate extravaganzas that will really wow moms. One year it was a chocolate jewelry box. Another year I created a pair of Manolo Blahniks, and then created a handbag to match those chocolate high heels. I know that anything chocolate will warm a mother's heart, but a flight of chocolate fancy will make it melt.

Savory Chocolate Napoleon

Makes 40

These chocolate napoleons are served as an hors d'oeuvre, rather than as dessert. A hint of Mexico can be tasted in the slightly spicy cream cheese filling. They are also perfect with a chocolate martini. I strongly urge you to use a bittersweet chocolate that has a cacao content of at least 72%. This will ensure that the napoleons are not too sweet and that they will have a good, strong chocolate flavor.

1 pound bittersweet chocolate, at least 72%, tempered (page 13)

1 pound cream cheese, softened

3 tablespoons chopped fresh chives

½ teaspoon hot paprika

½ teaspoon ancho chile powder

Pinch of salt

Pinch of freshly ground black pepper

Place a sheet of acetate on a clean, flat work surface. Pour the chocolate onto the acetate and, using an offset spatula, spread the chocolate evenly about ⅛ inch thick. Let stand for a few minutes, or just until the chocolate begins to set but is not yet hard.

Using a small, sharp knife or a rolling cutter (such as a pizza cutter), cut the chocolate into 1-inch squares. You should have about 120 squares. Let the chocolate stand for about 30 minutes, or until completely hardened. Peel the acetate off the chocolate, and carefully break the chocolate into squares. Set aside.

In the bowl of a stand mixer fitted with the paddle, combine the cream cheese, chives, paprika, chile powder, salt, and pepper and beat on medium speed for about 2 minutes, or just until combined.

Spoon the cream cheese mixture into a pastry bag fitted with a star tip. Pipe a ¾-inch dollop of cream cheese on a chocolate square. Top with a second chocolate square, and pipe a dollop of cheese onto it. Top with a final chocolate square. Repeat with the remaining squares and cream cheese mixture. As the napoleons are made, arrange them on a large, flat platter.

Serve immediately, or lightly cover the platter with plastic film and refrigerate until ready to serve, or for no more than 4 hours.

Chocolate Mousse

Serves 6

Although there are many versions of chocolate mousse, this simple adaptation has to be one of the best. It is so easy to make that you can easily memorize the recipe, which means that you can make it at the drop of a hat—or the drop-in of guests! I give two versions, bittersweet chocolate and white chocolate, which look fabulous piped together in a large, glass bowl. For the best results, be sure to chill both the mixer bowl for the cream and the bowl in which the cream and chocolate are blended. Although the mousse will keep, covered and refrigerated, for a couple of days, it is best when served shortly after making. The longer it sits, the heavier it becomes.

2 cups chilled heavy cream

7 ounces bittersweet chocolate, tempered (page 13)

Place the cream in the chilled bowl of a stand mixer fitted with the whip and beat on medium-high speed for about 4 minutes, or until soft peaks form.

Pour the chocolate into a stainless-steel bowl. Select a saucepan that will hold the bowl snugly in the rim. Fill the saucepan halfway with water and bring to a simmer. Place the bowl of chocolate over (not touching) the simmering water and heat to 120°F on a thermometer.

Slowly pour the whipped cream into the warm chocolate, whisking constantly just until combined. Scrape into a chilled bowl and continue to whisk until well blended.

Spoon into dessert cups or layer with White Chocolate Mousse (see the variation, below). Keep chilled until ready to serve.

VARIATION

White Chocolate Mousse: Follow the directions for Chocolate Mousse, substituting ¾ cup plus 2 tablespoons heavy cream for the 2 cups, and 13 ounces tempered white chocolate for the bittersweet chocolate. Heat the white chocolate to only 110°F.

Chocolate Hot Tamale

Makes 6 to 8 large cookies or about 4 dozen small cookies

The ancient Mexican tradition of adding warm spices to chocolate is one that I really love. I use traditional decorative wooden cookie molds to make these slightly spicy sweets. If you use them, be sure to press the dough firmly into the molds so that the pattern is deeply embedded and will be retained when the dough is baked. You can also cut out the dough with cookie cutters in any shape. The number of cookies the recipe yields depends on the size of the molds or cutters used.

These hot tamales are terrific with a cup of strong coffee or spicy hot chocolate (page 55).

½ cup (1 stick) unsalted butter,
at room temperature
—

2¾ cups cake flour
—

¾ cup confectioners' sugar
—

½ cup Dutch-processed cocoa
powder
—

¼ cup almond flour
—

Pinch of salt
—

Pinch of ancho chile powder
—

1 large egg, at room temperature
—

Preheat the oven to 350°F. Line a 15½-by-10½-by-1-inch nonstick baking sheet (jelly-roll or quarter sheet pan) with a silicone mat or parchment paper. Or lightly spray with nonstick baking spray. Set aside.

Place the butter in the bowl of a stand mixer fitted with the paddle and begin beating on low speed until the butter has softened. Add the cake flour and beat just until combined. Add the confectioners' sugar, cocoa powder, almond flour, salt, and chile powder and beat just until blended. Add the egg and mix for about 30 seconds, or just until combined.

Lay a piece of parchment paper on a clean, flat work surface. Scrape the dough from the bowl onto the parchment and pat into a disk. Using a rolling pin, roll out the dough about ¼ inch thick. (If using cookie cutters, scrape the dough onto a lightly floured work surface, pat into a disk, and roll out ¼ inch thick.)

Using a kitchen knife, cut the dough into squares about the size of your molds, so that the pieces can be easily fitted into the molds, and then press them into the molds. Tap the dough out of the molds onto the prepared baking sheet, spacing the cookies about 1 inch apart. (Or, cut out the dough with cookie cutters and transfer the cutouts to the baking sheet.)

Bake for about 20 minutes, or until firm and lightly browned around the edges.

Remove from the oven, transfer to wire racks, and let cool completely. Store, in an airtight container, for up to 1 week.

Chocolate Angel Food Cake

Makes one 10-inch cake

This classic American cake can be as simple as a cocoa-flavored low-fat dessert or as over-the-top as a beautifully decorated extravaganza complete with whipped cream, berries, and chocolate décor. The choice is yours! It is a wonderful Mother's Day dessert, either way.

You will need an angel food cake pan, which is a deep tube pan with a removable bottom, often with three small feet on the rim for standing the cake upside down to cool. (In the absence of the feet, you can invert the cake on the neck of a sturdy, long-necked bottle or a large metal funnel.) The pan must be absolutely squeaky clean, or the cake will fall as it bakes.

¾ cup sifted cake flour

½ cup Dutch-processed cocoa powder

1½ cups sifted superfine sugar

13 large egg whites, at room temperature

¼ teaspoon salt

1½ teaspoons cream of tartar

1 teaspoon pure vanilla extract

Chocolate Sauce (page 186), optional

1½ cups heavy cream, whipped, optional

3 cups raspberries, optional

Chocolate (any type) shavings, optional

Preheat the oven to 375°F. Have ready an ungreased 10-inch angel food cake pan.

Combine the flour, cocoa powder, and ¾ cup of the sugar and sift together three times. Set aside.

In the bowl of a stand mixer fitted with the whip, combine the egg whites and salt and beat on low speed just until foamy. Sprinkle the cream of tartar over the egg whites and continue to beat on low until blended. Raise the speed to medium-high and beat for about 4 minutes, or until soft peaks form. Do not overbeat. The peaks should hold their shape, but not be stiff.

Reduce the speed to medium, add the vanilla, and gradually sprinkle the remaining ¾ cup sugar over the egg whites, beating to incorporate. On low speed, add the flour mixture in three additions, mixing until incorporated after each addition and stopping the mixer after each addition to scrape down the sides and along the bottom of the bowl. You just want to make sure that the flour is evenly incorporated into the batter; you don't want to deflate it by beating.

Scrape the batter into the pan. Cut through the batter with a knife to eliminate any bubbles.

Bake for about 35 minutes, or until the top is lightly browned and a cake tester inserted into the center comes out clean. Remove from the oven and turn the pan upside down, standing it on its feet or resting it on the long neck of a heatproof bottle or large metal funnel. Let stand for about 2 hours, or until completely cool.

Turn the cake right side up, and carefully run a sharp knife around the inside edge of the pan to release the cake sides. Holding on to the tube portion, carefully lift the cake from the pan sides. Then run the knife between the tube and the cake and the bottom and the cake. Invert the cake onto a plate and tap it free. Brush off any loose crumbs with your hands.

For a simple dessert, slice the cake—use a serrated knife and a sawing motion—and serve each slice with a drizzle of Chocolate Sauce.

For a fancy dessert, using a serrated knife, carefully cut the cake horizontally into three equal layers. Place the bottom layer, cut side up, on a cake stand or serving plate. Spoon about ½ cup whipped cream onto the layer and spread with an offset spatula. Top with about 1 cup raspberries in a single layer. Add the middle layer, carefully spread it with about ½ cup whipped cream, and again top with about 1 cup raspberries. Place the third layer on top and coat the top and sides of the cake with the remaining whipped cream. Arrange the remaining raspberries decoratively on the top, and shave a few chocolate curls over all.

Refrigerate the cake until ready to serve, or for up to 6 hours. At serving time, using a serrated knife and a sawing motion, cut into individual slices and serve as is or drizzled with Chocolate Sauce.

Fours Pochés

Makes about 5 dozen

F*ours pochés* means "piped cookies" in French. These cookies are especially beautiful when the dough is made in both chocolate and vanilla flavors and then piped through a pastry bag into black and white stars. You can, of course, make just chocolate (using only the cocoa powder) or vanilla (using only the cornstarch), and the cookies will still be terrific. Include them in an assortment of petits fours for lunch or for tea.

2⅔ cups pastry flour

6 tablespoons Dutch-processed cocoa powder or cornstarch

1 cup plus 2 tablespoons unsalted butter, at room temperature

6 tablespoons confectioners' sugar

½ teaspoon salt

½ teaspoon pure vanilla extract

1½ (about 3 tablespoons) egg whites, at room temperature

Preheat the oven to 350°F. Line 2 cookie sheets with silicone mats or parchment paper.

In a small bowl, stir together the pastry flour and the cocoa powder, if you want chocolate cookies, or cornstarch, if you want vanilla cookies. Set aside.

In the bowl of a stand mixer fitted with the paddle, combine the butter, confectioners' sugar, salt, and vanilla and beat on medium speed for about 5 minutes, or until very light and airy. Slowly add the egg whites and beat until well incorporated. Remove the bowl from the mixer and, using a rubber spatula, fold in the flour mixture just until blended.

Spoon the dough into a pastry bag fitted with a large star tip. Pipe into star shapes about 1½ inches in diameter on the prepared baking sheets, spacing them about 1 inch apart.

Bake for about 12 minutes, or until lightly browned around the edges. Remove from the oven, transfer the cookies to wire racks, and let cool completely. Store, in an airtight container, at room temperature for up to 5 days.

Chocolate Crème Brûlée

Makes 6

In a few short years in the '80s, crème brûlée went from being virtually unknown in the United States to being a featured dessert on countless dessert menus. We can thank chef Dieter Schorner, the first pastry chef at Le Cirque restaurant, for introducing this classic French delight to American diners. I've developed this chocolate version, which is creamy-smooth and rich beneath its crisply crackling crust.

For a layered variation on this dessert, make a plain custard by replacing the melted chocolate with an additional 1 cup heavy cream and put about 2 tablespoons Chocolate Ganache (page 114) in the bottom of each dish before topping it with custard.

6 large egg yolks

1 large whole egg

¾ cup plus 2 tablespoons granulated sugar

3 cups heavy cream

1 cup (about 6 ounces) melted bittersweet chocolate

½ vanilla bean, split in half lengthwise

¾ cup packed light brown sugar

Preheat the oven to 300°F. Place 6 crème brûlée dishes, each 3 to 5 inches long and at least 1 inch deep, on a rimmed baking sheet.

In a bowl, whisk together the egg yolks, whole egg, and granulated sugar until well combined. Set aside.

In a heavy-bottomed saucepan, combine the cream and chocolate. Using the edge of a small, sharp knife, scrape the seeds from the vanilla bean into the pan and then add the bean. Place over medium heat, bring to a bare simmer, then remove from the heat.

Slowly pour the hot cream mixture into the egg mixture while whisking constantly. Continue to whisk until the mixture is well blended and smooth. Pour the mixture through a fine-mesh sieve into a large glass measuring cup with a pouring spout. (This measuring cup is not necessary, but it makes pouring the custard into the baking dishes quite a bit easier.)

Fill each crème brûlée dish about one-half full. Pull out the oven rack, place the baking sheet on the rack, and carefully fill each dish to the top with the remaining custard. Pour enough hot tap water into the baking sheet to come halfway up the sides of the filled dishes, and push in the oven rack. (If you have a convection oven, skip the water. The air circulation insulates the custards from the onslaught of direct heat and keeps them moist.)

Bake for 30 to 40 minutes, or until the custards tremble just a bit when a dish is gently moved. If you can see any liquid under the top skin, bake for an additional 5 minutes. Remove the pan from the oven, carefully transfer the dishes to wire racks, and let cool completely. Then cover and refrigerate for at least 3 hours or up to 3 days.

Three hours before serving, spread the brown sugar on a baking sheet and let sit at room temperature until dry and sandy. This is important, because if the sugar is wet, it won't glaze probably. When the sugar is dry, push it through a fine-mesh sieve to ensure it is lump free. Set aside.

When ready to serve, place the broiler pan about 4 inches from the heat source and preheat the broiler. Remove the custards from the refrigerator and sprinkle the tops evenly with the brown sugar, using about 2 tablespoons for each custard and covering the tops completely.

Place the custards under the broiler and broil, watching carefully, for about 90 seconds, or until the top is beautifully caramelized and glassy. Keep a sharp eye on the custards, as the sugar can burn very quickly. Alternately, you can caramelize the sugar with a hand-held butane kitchen torch by holding the flame about 2 inches from the surface and moving it slowly around to evenly melt the sugar, and color and set the top glaze. Remove from the broiler and serve immediately.

Esterel Cake

Makes one 8-inch cake

Some of my favorite cakes to make are the simple ones I learned in France. This one, made up of thin, tender cake layers sandwiching chocolate, raspberries and good-quality preserves, can be baked in advance and held in the refrigerator, making it a wonderful summer dinner-party dessert. The Esterel is an area between Cannes and Toulon where the ground is a beautiful red color. This cake, topped with bright red raspberrries, is named in honor of that red earth. Bring it to near room temperature before serving.

¾ cup blanched whole almonds

4 large whole eggs, at room temperature

1½ cups plus 2 tablespoons confectioners' sugar, plus more for dusting cake layers

5 large egg whites, at room temperature

2 tablespoons unsalted butter, melted and cooled

¼ cup pastry flour, sifted

7 ounces bittersweet chocolate, finely chopped

½ cup plus 2 tablespoons heavy cream

¼ cup good-quality raspberry jam

1 pint fresh raspberries

Preheat the oven to 400°F. Line two baking sheets (jelly-roll or quarter sheet pans) with parchment paper. Set aside.

Place the almonds in the bowl of a food processor fitted with the metal blade and process to a fine powder (almond flour). Be careful not to overprocess, or the oil in the nuts will be released, and a paste will form.

In the bowl of a stand mixer fitted with the paddle, combine the whole eggs, 1¼ cups of the confectioners' sugar, and the ground almonds and beat on medium-high speed for about 1 minute, or until light and creamy. Transfer to a bowl, thoroughly wash and dry the mixer bowl, and return it to the mixer. (If you have a handheld mixer, you can use it for this step and reserve the stand mixer for the meringue.)

In the bowl of the stand mixer fitted with the whip, beat the egg whites on medium speed until foamy. Raise the speed to medium-high and add the remaining 6 tablespoons confectioners' sugar, a bit at a time, beating constantly for about 4 minutes, or until stiff, but not dry, peaks form. Do not overwhip, or the meringue will be tough.

Remove the bowl from the mixer and, using a rubber spatula, fold the nut mixture into the meringue in two additions, taking care not to deflate the mixture by overmixing. Gently fold in the melted butter, followed by the flour, folding just to incorporate.

Using an offset spatula, evenly spread about two-thirds of the batter in one of the prepared pans, covering it completely. Evenly spread the remaining batter in the second prepared pan, shaping it into an 8-inch square in the center of the pan. (The offset spatula makes it easy to create even layers). Don't worry too much about the shape, as you can trim the cakes to equal sizes after they have baked.

Place a little confectioners' sugar in a fine-mesh sieve and, tapping on the side of the sieve, dust the top of each cake with the sugar. Bake for about 8 minutes, or until evenly browned around the edges and set in the center. Remove from the oven and immediately invert onto wire racks to cool. This is very important, as you don't want the cake to continue cooking in the pan. Let cool completely.

While the cakes are cooling (or about 1 hour before you are ready to assemble the final cake), prepare the ganache: Place the chocolate in a heatproof bowl. Place the cream in a small, heavy-bottomed saucepan over medium heat and heat just until distinct bubbles begin to form around the edges of the pan. Remove from the heat and slowly pour the hot cream over the chocolate. Let stand for 30 seconds, until the chocolate begins to melt, then begin beating with a wooden spoon until smooth. Set aside for a bit less than 1 hour, or until the ganache reaches a spreading consistency. Do not refrigerate to speed the process, or the ganache will be too firm to spread.

To assemble the cake, peel the parchment off of the 2 cakes. Using a serrated knife, cut the large cake into two equal squares and trim the smaller cake to a size equal to the other two cakes. You should now have 3 cake layers of equal size, about 7½ inches square.

Place 1 cake layer on a cake plate or serving tray. Spoon about half of the ganache on the layer and spread evenly with an offset spatula to cover completely to the edge. Top with a second cake layer. Spoon the raspberry jam on the layer and spread evenly to cover completely to the edge. Top with the final cake layer, spoon the remaining ganache on top, and again spread evenly to cover completely. Because this is the top layer, it is important that it be very even. Transfer the cake to the refrigerator for at least 1 hour or up to 6 hours. Remove the cake from the refrigerator and arrange the raspberries on top in a decorative pattern. Cut into slices and serve.

Chocolate Sticky Buns

Makes 7 buns

Every Saturday morning, the smell of these sticky buns baking fills the shop. We usually have to make a couple of extra batches, as all of the staff loves them, including me. A bit different than the standard sticky buns, I use a brioche dough, rum raisins, and chocolate for an interesting combination of flavors. You can easily make them the night before and refrigerate the unbaked rolls. Then, pop them in the oven for an early-morning treat or as the perfect breakfast-in-bed for Mom.

2 cups bread flour

3 tablespoons granulated sugar

1¼ teaspoons salt

2 envelopes (2½ teaspoons each) active dry yeast

2 large eggs

⅓ cup water

6 tablespoons unsalted butter, chilled and cubed

½ cup light brown sugar

½ cup finely chopped bittersweet chocolate

1¼ tablespoons ground cinnamon

Walnut Topping (recipe follows)

¼ cup melted unsalted butter

Combine the flour, 2 tablespoons of the granulated sugar, and salt in the bowl of a stand mixer fitted with the dough hook. Add the yeast. Whisk the eggs and water together and then pour the egg mixture into the flour mixture. Begin mixing on low just until the wet and dry ingredients combine. Raise the speed to medium and continue to beat for about 4 minutes, or until the dough becomes homogenous and holds together.

Add all of the cubed butter and raise the speed to medium-high. Beat for about 5 minutes, or until the dough is smooth and elastic.

Lightly flour a smooth work surface. Using a rubber spatula, scrape the dough out onto it and pat the dough into a disk. Let rest for 30 minutes.

Wrap the dough disk in plastic film and place in the refrigerator for at least 2 hours or overnight to allow the butter to chill into the dough. This will make the dough much easier to work with.

Combine the remaining granulated sugar with the brown sugar, chocolate, and cinnamon in a small mixing bowl.

Lightly butter a 9-inch round cake pan that is at least 3 inches deep. Place the Walnut Topping in the bottom of the pan, spreading it out to cover entirely. Set aside.

Lightly flour a clean, flat work surface. Unwrap the chilled dough and place it in the center of the floured surface. Using a rolling pin, lightly roll the dough out to a rectangle about 14 by 10 inches. Using a pastry brush, generously coat the dough with the melted butter. Leaving about ½ inch uncovered on the longer edge at the top of the dough, sprinkle the sugar mixture over the dough. Begin rolling the rectangle into a firm log shape, ending with the uncovered edge. Gently press the edge into the roll.

Using a sharp knife, cut the log into 7 equal rounds. Place 6 of the rounds in a circular shape around the edge of the pan with their edges touching. Place the remaining round in the center of the pan. Cover with plastic film and set aside to rise for 1 hour, or until doubled in bulk.

Preheat the oven to 350°F.

Uncover the rolls and place in the preheated oven. Bake for about 25 minutes, or until golden brown.

Remove from the oven and let rest for about 10 minutes, or until slightly cool. Invert the pan, releasing the buns. Serve warm.

Walnut Topping

¾ cup light brown sugar
——

¾ cup walnut pieces
——

5 tablespoons melted unsalted butter
——

Place the brown sugar and walnuts in a small mixing bowl. Add the melted butter and stir to blend.

Use as directed in the recipe.

JUNE

Graduations, Weddings, and a Day for Dad

When I was a pastry chef, June was a month of cakes. I didn't mind the special graduation cakes requested by proud parents, but wedding cakes were my nemesis. It wasn't that I couldn't do them or wouldn't do them. It was that I didn't want to do them. You might wonder why, since these monoliths of patisserie would seem to be a pastry chef's dream. The reason is simple: I like to create my own monuments, and every bride-to-be (along with her mother, future mother-in-law, girlfriends, friends, and the groom-to-be) has a definite idea about how the wedding cake should look and taste. As much as I wish every couple headed down the aisle all the good luck in the world, I don't want to be entangled in the family arguments that too often play a major part in planning the "big day."

Second wedding cakes, on the other hand, are high on my list. Only recently did I discover that over half of all weddings today are for the second time around, so I guess other people like them as much as I do. This is where the fun is! The bride and groom are often the only people involved in the planning, and they are ready to celebrate. No white pyramids, no décor to match the dress, no demands—just "make us a cake that everyone will eat." And, occasionally, even with the chocolate factory running full steam, I do—just for the fun of it.

I am amazed at the ingenuity of both marriage planners and brides. Everyone wants their guests to take home a special memento of the occasion and will go to the extreme to make their wish a reality. Every June, a number of our chocolate treats provide a take-home memory of the special event, as brides and their friends gather before the big day to assemble their specialty wedding favors.

Chocolate Tarts

Cloud Puffs

Spiced Chocolate Sugar Cookies

Chocolate Crème Anglaise

Profiteroles

Langues de Chat

Chocolate Pound Cake

Brownies

Graduations also seem to bring requests for chocolate tributes. For these occasions, I make a molded chocolate mortar board and diploma that are always a big hit with graduates, from nursery school to college. Looking for inspiration, I once checked the Internet to see what the most popular graduation presents were and I found that money topped the list (understandable), so I molded a few chocolate bucks. Not as good as the real thing, I know, but they do make everyone happy. I have also made the perennial favorite fountain pen gift in chocolate, although, with computers, I don't think anyone uses a real one anymore.

And last, but not least, comes Dad. For him, just like for Mom in May, we need something very special. I have made chocolate ties, socks, wallets, and various pieces of sports equipment, but my all-time favorite gift for dads is a chocolate tool chest spilling over with chocolate tools.

Since June is a time of so many special milestones in life that call for entertaining friends and family, I have gathered an assortment of chocolate goodies that are particularly suited to grand events. Although they might take a bit more preparation, each one will rise to the occasion.

Chocolate Tarts

Makes 6

These sophisticated little tarts can be made with any pastry, but I particularly like the combination of rich chocolate and tasty nut pastry. You can decorate them any way you like. They are delicious with just a dollop of whipped cream and a sprinkling of nuts, but you can take them to new heights with some fanciful chocolate decorations nestled into the whipped cream.

8 ounces bittersweet chocolate, finely chopped

1 teaspoon finely grated orange zest

1 cup heavy cream

2½ tablespoons honey

6 tablespoons unsalted butter, at room temperature, cut into pieces

6 baked Nut Pastry tart shells (recipe follows)

Whipped cream for garnish, optional

Candied orange zest or chopped toasted nuts for garnish, optional

Place the chocolate and grated orange zest in a heatproof mixing bowl. Set aside.

Combine the cream and honey in a medium heavy-bottomed saucepan over medium heat. Heat just until bubbles form around the edge of the pan. Immediately remove from the heat and pour half of the mixture over the chocolate. Let stand for 30 seconds and then whisk to blend. Add the remaining hot cream and again let stand for 30 seconds. Then beat until smooth. Add the butter and beat to blend.

Pour an equal portion of the chocolate mixture into each tart shell, carefully smoothing the top with an offset spatula. Transfer to the refrigerator and let chill for at least 1½ hours or up to 6 hours before serving.

Serve chilled, garnished with candied orange zest or chopped nuts and a dollop of whipped cream, if desired.

Nut Pastry

1½ cups all-purpose flour

———

1 cup finely ground walnuts, pecans, hazelnuts, or almonds

———

1½ tablespoons sugar

———

1 teaspoon cold unsalted butter

———

2 large egg yolks, beaten

———

2 teaspoons ice water, if needed

———

Combine the flour, nuts, and sugar in a mixing bowl. Using a fork, cut in the butter to just blend. Stir in the egg yolks, mixing with the fork just until the dough comes together. If necessary, add ice water, a few drops at a time.

Form the dough into a ball and wrap in plastic film. Refrigerate for 1 hour, or until thoroughly chilled.

When ready to roll out, lightly flour a clean, flat work surface.

Preheat the oven to 350°F.

Lightly butter six 4-inch round fluted tart pans with a removable bottom.

Remove the dough from the refrigerator and unwrap it. Place it on the lightly floured surface and, using a rolling pin, roll out to a circle about ⅛ inch thick.

Using a plain or fluted 5-inch round cutter, cut 6 dough circles. Working with one at a time, fit a pastry round into each tart shell, pressing it into the bottom and sides. Work carefully, as the dough is a bit fragile. If it breaks, just push it together with your fingertips. Even the edge of the pastry with the rim of the pan.

Place the tart shells on a baking sheet and bake for about 10 minutes, or until lightly browned. Remove from the oven and place on wire racks to cool until ready to fill.

Cloud Puffs

Makes about 20 dozen

*I*f you think that popcorn is addictive, just wait until you make these ethereal fritters. You'll be popping them into your mouth as soon as they emerge from the sugar-coating. Light as air, sweet as love, and chocolate, too—what more could you want from dessert? Cloud Puffs are perfect for almost any time of the year.

1 cup plus pinch of granulated sugar

———

1 cup water

———

½ cup plus 1 tablespoon unsalted butter, cut into pieces

———

Pinch of salt

———

1 cup bread flour

———

¼ cup Dutch-processed cocoa powder

———

2 or 3 large eggs, at room temperature

———

6 cups vegetable oil for deep-frying

———

1 cup confectioners' sugar

———

Line 2 rimmed baking sheets with a triple layer of paper towels. Place 1 cup of the granulated sugar in a large bowl. Set aside.

In a heavy-bottomed saucepan, combine the water, butter, the remaining pinch of sugar, and the salt and bring to a boil over medium-high heat. Boil for 1 to 2 minutes, or until the butter has melted.

Remove from the heat and immediately add the flour and cocoa powder, beating with a wooden spoon to incorporate. Return the pan to medium heat and cook for about 3 minutes, using a wooden spoon to turn the batter up and into itself to help dry it out. You must keep continual motion so that the mixture does not stick and burn. The dough is sufficiently dry when it leaves a thin layer on the bottom of the pan. Immediately remove the pans from the heat.

Transfer the paste to the bowl of a stand mixer fitted with the paddle. Mix on low speed for about 2 minutes to cool slightly. Add 2 eggs, one at a time, beating after each addition until well incorporated. The paste may appear to separate after each addition, but it will come back together as the egg is incorporated into it. The dough should be smooth, pale yellow, slightly elastic, moist, and sticky. Add the additional egg if necessary to achieve this consistency.

Pour the oil into a deep-fryer or a heavy-bottomed saucepan with a basket insert and heat to 330°F. It is important to maintain this heat because if the oil is too hot, the puffs will brown too quickly and be raw inside; if it is not hot enough, the dough will absorb too much of the fat before it is fully cooked.

Scrape the batter into a pastry bag fitted with a ½-inch plain tip. Dip a bamboo skewer (or other long, thin implement) into the hot oil and then place or hold it across the top of the pan. Holding the pastry bag over the hot oil, begin piping ½-inch-long pieces of batter into the oil, using the skewer to cut the batter to the proper length as you pipe. The batter won't stick to the oiled skewer, plus the skewer ensures that the batter falls directly into the hot oil. Continue piping until the pan is full but not overcrowded, keeping in mind that the batter will puff up as it cooks.

Fry for about 5 minutes, or until lightly colored and puffed up. Use a slotted spoon to turn the puffs as they fry to ensure that all sides are cooked and colored evenly. Then, using the slotted spoon, transfer the cooked puffs to the prepared baking sheets to drain. Repeat until all of the batter has been fried.

While the puffs are still warm, roll them in the granulated sugar, coating well. Then, just before serving, place the confectioners' sugar in a fine-mesh sieve and, tapping the side of the sieve, lightly dust all of the puffs. Serve while still warm.

Spiced Chocolate Sugar Cookies

Makes about 4 dozen cookies

Spice and chocolate is one of my favorite combinations. These cookies are crisp on the outside and chewy and moist on the inside—perfect for dipping into a cool glass of milk or for just snacking on at picnic time.

1 ¾ cups all-purpose flour

2 teaspoons baking soda

1 teaspoon ground cinnamon

¼ teaspoon ancho chile powder

¼ teaspoon salt

½ cup (1 stick) unsalted butter

1 cup packed dark brown sugar

1 large egg

2 ounces unsweetened chocolate, melted and cooled

¼ cup light corn syrup

1 cup (about 6 ounces) chopped bittersweet chocolate

¼ cup granulated sugar

Preheat the oven to 350°F. Line 2 cookie sheets with parchment paper or silicone mats. Set aside.

In a bowl, sift together the flour, baking soda, cinnamon, chile powder, and salt. Set aside. In the bowl of a stand mixer fitted with the paddle, beat the butter on low speed to soften. Add the brown sugar, raise the speed to medium, and beat until well blended. Add the egg and beat until incorporated. Add the melted chocolate and corn syrup and beat until blended. Reduce the speed to low, add the flour mixture, and beat for about 3 minutes, or until a stiff dough forms. Remove the bowl from the mixer and, using a rubber spatula, fold in the chopped chocolate.

Spread the granulated sugar on a small plate. To shape the cookies, scoop up a nugget of the dough, form it into a 1-inch ball between your palms, and roll the ball in the granulated sugar to coat evenly. Place the sugared balls on the prepared cookie sheets, spacing them about 2 inches apart.

Bake for about 12 minutes, or until the cookies have puffed up and the tops are cracked. Remove from the oven, let cool on the pans on wire racks for 5 minutes, then transfer to wire racks and let cool completely.

Serve immediately, or arrange in a single layer in 1 or more airtight containers and store at room temperature for up to 3 days.

Chocolate Crème Anglaise

Makes about 1 ½ cups

This is a chocolate version of the classic French dessert sauce. Served hot or cold, it will turn a plain piece of cake or fresh fruit into a special after-dinner treat. It is perfect to keep on hand for last-minute entertaining. It's a great recipe for summer months when you don't want to add too much heat to the kitchen.

7 large egg yolks

½ cup plus 1 tablespoon sugar

2 ¼ cups whole milk

½ cup heavy cream

1 vanilla bean, split in half lengthwise

5 ounces bittersweet chocolate, finely chopped

Place the egg yolks in a bowl, and whisk them to break them up. Add ¼ cup of the sugar and whisk until thick, smooth, and well blended. Set aside.

In a heavy-bottomed saucepan, combine the milk and cream. Using the edge of a small, sharp knife, scrape the seeds from the vanilla bean into the milk mixture and then add the bean. Place over medium heat, bring to a boil, then immediately remove from the heat.

Whisking constantly, whisk about one-third of the hot milk mixture into the egg yolk mixture. Pour the combined mixtures into the hot milk, whisk to combine, and return to medium heat. Cook, stirring constantly with a heatproof rubber spatula, for about 7 minutes, or until thick enough to coat the back of a spoon (about 182°F). Do not allow the mixture to come to a boil, or it will curdle.

Remove from the heat and whisk in the chocolate until melted and smooth. Pour through a fine-mesh sieve into a clean container. Use immediately, or let cool, stirring occasionally.

Cover with plastic film, pressing it directly onto the surface to keep a skin from forming. Refrigerate until ready to use or for up to 3 days.

Profiteroles

Serves 4

Profiteroles, ice cream–filled choux puffs, are a favorite all over the world. Though you might think these fancy desserts are difficult to make, profiteroles are relatively simple to prepare. Vanilla is the usual ice cream used, but no one says that you can't use any flavor you like. I particularly like coffee ice cream. If you want to make this dessert extra special, decorate it with chocolate shavings or, better yet, a chocolate fan (page 37) or two.

1 ¼ cups water

½ cup (1 stick) plus 1 tablespoon unsalted butter, cubed

1 teaspoon sugar

1 teaspoon salt

1 ¼ cups bread flour

¼ cup Dutch-process cocoa powder

5 or 6 large eggs

4 large scoops Vanilla Ice Cream (page 122)

Chocolate Sauce (page 186), warmed

Preheat the oven to 400°F. Line 2 rimmed baking sheets with parchment paper. Set aside.

To make the choux paste for the puffs, combine the water, butter, sugar, and salt in a heavy-bottomed saucepan and bring to a boil over medium-high heat. Boil for 1 to 2 minutes, or until the butter has melted.

Remove from the heat and immediately add the flour and cocoa powder all at once, beating well with a wooden spoon to incorporate. Return the pan to medium heat and cook, stirring vigorously with the spoon, for about 3 minutes, or until some of the liquid has evaporated and the paste has dried out somewhat. The dough is sufficiently dry when it leaves a thin layer on the bottom of the pan. Immediately remove the pan from the heat.

Transfer the choux paste to the bowl of a stand mixer fitted with the paddle. Beat on low speed for 2 minutes to release some of the moist heat. Then, with the mixer still on low speed, begin adding the eggs, one at a time, beating after each addition until well incorporated. The number of eggs added will depend on how dry the paste was before the additions began. The drier the mix, the more eggs required. Begin testing for the correct consistency after the fourth egg has been added. Scoop a large amount of the paste onto a wooden spoon. Hold the spoon horizontally about a foot above the bowl and then allow the paste to fall off the spoon, watching carefully. If the paste is very smooth but moist, pale yellow, slightly sticky, and elastic, and takes 5 to 7 seconds to fall, it is ready. If not, add another egg and test again. The correct consistency is important because if the paste is too dry, it won't pipe, and if it is too wet, it won't hold its shape.

Scrape the paste into a pastry bag fitted with a ½-inch plain tip. Begin piping 2½-inch rounds about 1½ inches apart onto the prepared baking sheets. This recipe calls for only 4 pastry puffs, but you will be able to make about 20 pastries with this amount of paste.

You can freeze any unbaked pastries on the baking sheet until completely frozen, transfer them to a resealable plastic bag, label, and freeze for up to 3 weeks. When ready to bake, return to a parchment-lined baking sheet, thaw in the refrigerator for 1 hour, then bake as directed. Or, you can bake them all and store, airtight, up for to 3 days.

Bake for 15 minutes. Lower the oven temperature to 375°F and continue to bake for an additional 15 minutes, or until well puffed, dry, and golden brown. To help the puffs dry, you can open the oven door during the last 5 minutes of baking to allow steam to escape. Remove from the oven, transfer to wire racks, and let cool completely before filling.

When ready to assemble, using a sharp knife, split 4 puffs in half crosswise. Place a scoop of ice cream in the bottom of each puff. Place the top on at a slight angle.

Cover the bottom of each dessert plate with a pool of warm Chocolate Sauce. Place an ice cream–filled puff in the center of each pool. Drizzle more warm sauce over the top and serve at once.

Langues de Chat

Makes about 4 dozen sandwiched cookies

Known as cat's tongues in English, these cookies are one of the first cookies that a young French pastry chef learns to make. They got their name because of their long, delicate shape. Turn them into sandwich cookies by pressing them together with jam, or leave them plain, lovely at teatime.

These cookies bake best on nonstick baking sheets. If you don't have them, lightly butter and flour regular baking sheets.

½ cup (1 stick) unsalted butter, at room temperature

1 cup plus 2 tablespoons confectioners' sugar

1 vanilla bean, split in half lengthwise

4 large egg whites, at room temperature

1 cup pastry flour

1 cup good-quality raspberry jam

12 ½ ounces bittersweet chocolate, tempered (page 13)

In the bowl of a stand mixer fitted with the paddle, combine the butter and confectioners' sugar and beat on medium speed for about 5 minutes, or until very creamy. Using the edge of a small, sharp knife, scrape the seeds from the vanilla bean into the creamed mixture. Continue to beat the mixture for about 5 minutes longer, or until it increases in volume and is very pale.

Add 2 of the egg whites and beat just until combined. Add half of the flour and beat just until blended. Add the remaining 2 egg whites and beat until well blended. Add the remaining flour and beat just until incorporated. Do not overbeat, or the cookies will be tough.

Scrape the dough into a pastry bag fitted with a ¼-inch plain tip. Set aside at room temperature to rest for 1 hour.

Preheat the oven to 350°F. Have ready at least 2 nonstick cookie sheets.

Pressing evenly and gently on the pastry bag, pipe 2 ½-inch-long lines about 1 inch apart on the baking sheets.

Bake for about 6 minutes, or until lightly browned around the edges. Remove from the oven, let cool on the pans on wire racks for 2 minutes, then transfer to wire racks and let cool completely.

Place sheets of parchment paper on a clean, flat work surface. Working with 2 cookies at a time, carefully and neatly spread a layer of jam on the flat side of 1 cookie and then top it, flat side down, with the second cookie. Place on the parchment paper.

Place the chocolate in a warmed bowl. One at a time, dip the sandwiched cookies halfway and on the diagonal into the chocolate, allowing the excess chocolate to drip back into the bowl. Lay the finished cookies on the parchment paper and let stand for about 15 minutes, or until completely hardened.

Serve immediately, or layer the cookies, separated by sheets of waxed paper, in an airtight container and store at room temperature for up to 3 days.

Chocolate Pound Cake

Makes two 10-inch loaf cakes

This really isn't a traditional pound cake—a pound each of butter, sugar, eggs, and flour—but it is light as a feather and as easy as one-two-three to make. I use extra eggs to keep the cake moist, so it stays fresh tasting for a few days. Here, I bake two cakes in loaf pans, but you can also bake the cake in a large Bundt pan.

10 large egg yolks, at room temperature

——

5 large whole eggs, at room temperature

——

2 ½ cups cake flour, sifted

——

½ cup Dutch-processed cocoa powder, sifted

——

1 tablespoon plus 1 teaspoon baking powder

——

1 pound (4 sticks) unsalted butter, at room temperature

——

1 ¾ cups sugar

——

2 tablespoons honey

——

1 vanilla bean, split in half lengthwise

——

Preheat the oven to 350°F. Lightly butter two 10-by-5-inch loaf pans, or coat with nonstick baking spray.

In a small bowl, whisk together the egg yolks and whole eggs until blended. Set aside. In another bowl, sift together the flour, cocoa powder, and baking powder. Set aside.

In the bowl of a stand mixer fitted with the paddle, combine the butter, sugar, and honey and beat on medium-high speed for about 10 minutes, or until the mixture is very pale and has increased in volume. Using the edge of a small, sharp knife, scrape the seeds from the vanilla bean into the mixture and beat to combine.

Reduce the speed to medium-low and add the eggs one-third at a time alternately with the flour mixture one-third at a time, beating after each addition just until incorporated. After the final addition, beat the batter until smooth.

Using a rubber spatula, scrape the batter into the prepared pans, dividing it evenly. Bake for about 40 minutes, or until a cake tester inserted in the center comes out clean and the cakes are lightly colored around the edges. Remove from the oven and invert onto wire racks. Turn the cakes right side up and let cool completely.

Serve immediately, or wrap tightly and store in the refrigerator for up to 3 days or the freezer for up to 1 month.

Brownies

Makes about 35

Like chocolate chip cookies, every cook seems to have a favorite brownie recipe. And like chocolate chip cookies, brownies are a quintessential American sweet. I can't get enough of them! I like to add heft to the brownies by melting some of the chocolate and then adding the remainder in solid pieces. I also like the extra hit of chocolate that a top layer of ganache adds, but the brownies are still quite good without it.

12 ounces 72% bittersweet chocolate, chopped

¼ cup Dutch-processed cocoa powder

1 ¾ cups all-purpose flour

1 tablespoon baking powder

1 ½ teaspoons salt

1 ½ cups (3 sticks) unsalted butter, at room temperature

3 cups sugar

6 large eggs, at room temperature

10 ½ ounces 60% bittersweet chocolate, chopped

2 ⅔ cups walnuts, toasted and chopped

Chocolate Ganache (recipe follows), optional

Preheat the oven to 350°F. Line a 15 ½-by-10 ½-by-1-inch baking sheet (jelly-roll or quarter sheet pan) with parchment paper or a silicone mat, or lightly spray it with nonstick vegetable spray.

Place the 72% chocolate in the top half of a double boiler. Place over (not touching) gently simmering water in the bottom pan and heat, stirring occasionally, until completely melted. Remove from the heat and beat in the cocoa powder until well blended. Set aside.

In a bowl, sift together the flour, baking powder, and salt. Set aside.

In the bowl of a stand mixer fitted with the paddle, beat the butter on low speed until softened. Raise the speed to medium and beat for about 3 minutes, or until creamy. Add the sugar and continue beating for about 4 minutes, or until light and fluffy. Add the eggs one at a time, beating well after each addition until incorporated. Add the chocolate mixture and beat just until combined. Add the flour mixture and beat just until incorporated.

Remove the bowl from the mixer and, using a rubber spatula, fold in the 60% chocolate and the nuts. Scrape the batter into the prepared pan, lightly smoothing the top with the spatula.

Bake for about 30 minutes, or until cooked through. To test, push the top with your hand. It should feel about as firm as your palm. If you, like me, like your brownies a bit fudgy, it is important that they not be overbaked. Remove from the oven, place the pan on a wire rack, and let cool completely.

Lay a piece of parchment paper on a clean, flat surface. Run a paring knife around the edge of the pan to loosen the brownies from the sides of the pan. Invert the pan onto the parchment and tap the bottom to release the brownies, then lift off the pan. If the pan has a silicone or parchment lining, peel it away.

If using, spoon the ganache onto the center of the brownies. Using an offset spatula, smooth the ganache out to the edges, taking care to neaten all of the edges. Set aside for about 30 minutes, or until the ganache has set.

Using a sharp knife, cut the brownies into the desired size. I like cutting them into 2-inch squares. Serve immediately, or arrange in a single layer in an airtight container and store in a cool spot for up to 5 days. Or, wrap individually in plastic film, pack in resealable plastic bags, and freeze for up to 3 months.

NOTE: You can adjust the texture of the brownies by altering the ingredients. For soft, dense, fudgy brownies, use 2 parts cake flour and 1 part bread flour. For chewy brownies, use 2 parts bread flour and 1 part cake flour. Using melted butter in place of the room-temperature butter keeps the batter from rising, and the cooked brownies will be moist and dense (simply add the melted butter to the initial melted chocolate–cocoa mixture). Creamed butter encourages the batter to rise and results in brownies that are more crumbly. The more sugar you use, the drier and crispier the brownies will be. Corn syrup (added in a ratio of 1 to 3 with the sugar) will add moisture. And an extra egg yolk will make the brownies as cakey as they can be.

Chocolate Ganache

Makes about 2½ cups

8 ½ ounces 60% bittersweet chocolate, chopped

——

1 cup heavy cream

——

Place the chocolate in a heatproof bowl. Place the cream in a small, heavy-bottomed saucepan over medium heat and heat just until distinct bubbles begin to form around the edges of the pan. Remove from the heat and slowly pour about half of the hot cream over the chocolate. Let stand for 30 seconds, until the chocolate begins to melt. Then, using a wooden spoon, begin beating the mixture. As the mixture starts to smooth out, add the remaining cream and continue to beat until the mixture is very smooth.

Set aside to cool for about 15 minutes, or until set and creamy (it should be about the consistency of toothpaste).

JULY & AUGUST

Fourth of July, Bastille Day, and Picnics

July is one of my favorite months, as I get to celebrate the independence of my American homeland on the Fourth of July, and the *Fête nationale* or *14 juillet* (or Bastille Day, as it is known in the States) in the land of my childhood on the fourteenth of July. It is interesting that both countries celebrate in much the same way—fireworks, parades, and picnics are always part of the festivities.

I particularly love fireworks. New York is the site of a grand fireworks display on the East River, which ends with a thundering crash filling the sky with stars, stripes, and other symbols of Americana. As a child in France, I watched the fireworks over the Bay of Bandol in Provence, where every bang and flourish was exciting.

In France, the parades usually have a military theme, while in America they are more relaxed and have more community spirit. I have often spent summer weekends in Michigan and I love the small-town parades that I have seen there. Everyone participates, from Cub Scouts, Brownies, and rosy-cheeked 4-H kids to military veterans being pushed along in wheelchairs. Families gather for backyard celebrations or lakeside picnics. The picnic fare is amazingly bountiful—much more than the expected hot dogs and hamburgers—with salads, sandwiches, barbecued meats, and oh so many desserts. These gatherings are where I first discovered chocolate chip cookies and brownies. I feel so welcome and so American at these homey get-togethers. They are everything I ever imagined about life in small-town America.

In France, *14 juillet* is often celebrated in small towns with a community picnic. Families pack their individual baskets, but everyone meets in a park, along a stream or river's edge, or in the town square to observe the national holiday with communal spirit. The foods are usually quite simple and are always accompanied by a bottle or two of table wine. In the south, the wine is typically a chilled rosé, still one of my favorite drinks to toast national honor.

To celebrate the holiday, New York, and the American icon, I always make a molded chocolate Statue of Liberty candy bar, because the statue is both the international symbol of freedom and democracy and a dramatic representation of the friendship between the people of France and the United States. What better way for a French American to acknowledge his heritage and his home?

Chocolate Chip Cookies

———

Ice Cream Sundae

———

Chocolate Cupcakes

———

Chocolate Almond Cake

———

Chocolate-Covered Cereal

———

Chocolate Lollipops

Chocolate Chip Cookies

Makes 3 dozen large cookies

We feature these cookies all year long in our stores because they are so good, but I think they're best of all in the summer. We use them to make big, fat ice cream sandwiches filled with our homemade vanilla, coffee, raspberry, strawberry, peanut butter, or chocolate ice cream. They are also a perennial picnic-basket favorite.

I don't think that I had ever eaten a chocolate chip cookie until I came to the States. But I sure have eaten my share since my arrival. Everybody seems to have a favorite recipe: some with nuts, some with added candies, some with mixed chocolate pieces. This is my basic recipe.

Apparently the original Toll House cookie was made much as I now make mine: a cut-up chocolate bar added to a butter-rich cookie dough. No need for any improvement! However, if you like, you can customize these cookies to make them your own: For chocolate chocolate chip cookies, replace 1 cup of the flour with Dutch-processed cocoa

powder. For a cakelike texture, replace 1 of the eggs with 2 egg yolks. For very moist cookies, replace 5 ½ tablespoons of the brown sugar and ½ cup of the granulated sugar with an equal amount of light corn syrup. And, of course, you can always add nuts (pecans, macadamias, or walnuts); raisins or other sweet dried fruits, such as cherries or cranberries; or candy bits.

4 ¾ cups all-purpose flour

2 teaspoons salt

1 ½ teaspoons baking powder

1 ½ teaspoons baking soda

1 ½ cups (3 sticks) unsalted butter, at room temperature

2 ¼ cups packed light brown sugar

1 ¼ cups plus 2 ½ tablespoons granulated sugar

3 large eggs, at room temperature, lightly beaten

2 teaspoons pure vanilla extract

1 ⅔ pounds bittersweet chocolate, chopped into bite-sized pieces

Preheat the oven to 325°F. Have ready 2 nonstick cookie sheets, or line 2 regular cookie sheets with parchment paper or silicone mats. Set aside.

In a bowl, stir together the flour, salt, baking powder, and baking soda. Set aside. In the bowl of a stand mixer fitted with the paddle, beat the butter on medium speed for about 5 minutes, or until very light and fluffy Add the brown and granulated sugars and beat until well blended. Add the eggs and beat just until incorporated. Beat in the vanilla. Reduce the speed to low and add the flour mixture a little at a time, beating after each addition until incorporated. When all of the flour mixture has been incorporated, remove the bowl from the mixer and, using a rubber spatula, fold in the chocolate.

To shape the cookies, using a tablespoon, scoop out a heaping spoonful of the dough and, using the palms of your hands, form it into a 3-inch ball. Place the balls on the prepared baking sheets, spacing them about 1 inch apart.

Bake for about 15 minutes, or until lightly browned around the edges. Remove from the oven, transfer the cookies to wire racks, and let cool completely.

Store, in an airtight container, for up to 5 days.

NOTE: If you want to make ice cream sandwiches, prepare at least 6 sandwiches at a time and store them in the freezer so that you have them on hand for a quick treat. To make the sandwiches, allow whatever flavor ice cream (see pages 122 through 124 for recipes for vanilla, strawberry, and chocolate) you are going to use to soften slightly, planning on about 1 cup for each sandwich. Place 6 cookies, flat side up, on a parchment-lined baking sheet large enough to hold the sandwiches and small enough to fit in the freezer. Spoon the softened ice cream into a pastry bag fitted with a large fluted tip, and carefully pipe and swirl an equal portion of ice cream on top of each cookie. Place another cookie, flat side down, on top of the ice cream. Don't press down too hard, or the ice cream will ooze out. Immediately transfer the baking sheet to the freezer and freeze for about 1 hour, or until very firm. Then carefully wrap the sandwiches individually in plastic film for longer storage. They will keep for up to 3 months. Before eating, take the sandwiches out of the freezer and let them stand for a bit at room temperature to soften.

Ice Cream Sundae

Serves 1

The ice cream recipes that follow should give you enough ice cream to make a minimum of four sundaes. The instructions here, however, are for one sundae. The great thing about a sundae is that you can make it any way you want. All vanilla, all chocolate, whipped cream or not, nuts or no nuts, strawberries or bananas or no fruit, chocolate sauce, caramel sauce—you name it, it is yours to do. I'm particularly partial to chocolate ice cream with chocolate sauce and a sprinkle of chocolate-coated nuts.

1 scoop each Vanilla, Strawberry, and Chocolate Ice Cream (recipes follow)

¼ cup Chocolate Sauce (page 186), plus more for drizzling

1 cup whipped cream

¼ cup chopped Chocolate-Covered Almond Clusters (page 33)

Place the ice cream in a long, shallow sundae dish or other long, shallow dish. Spoon the ¼ cup sauce over the ice cream. Top with whipped cream and drizzle with additional sauce. Sprinkle chopped nuts over all. Serve before it melts!

Vanilla Ice Cream

Makes about 3 cups

⅔ cup sugar

———

7 large egg yolks

———

2 cups plus 1 tablespoon whole milk

———

½ cup heavy cream

———

1 ½ tablespoons honey

———

1 vanilla bean, split in half lengthwise

———

Place ¼ cup plus 1 tablespoon of the sugar in a large bowl. Whisk in the egg yolks, beating until well combined and the mixture is thick and smooth.

In a heavy-bottomed saucepan, combine the remaining sugar, the milk, cream, and honey. Using the edge of a small, sharp knife, scrape the seeds from the vanilla bean into the pan and then add the bean. Place over medium-high heat and bring to a boil, stirring occasionally. Immediately remove from the heat.

Slowly pour about one-third of the hot milk mixture into the egg yolk mixture, whisking constantly to temper the yolks. Pour the tempered egg mixture into the remaining hot milk mixture and, stirring constantly with a heatproof rubber spatula, place over medium heat. It should immediately begin to thicken. Cook for about 5 minutes, or until the mixture reaches 182°F on an instant-read thermometer and is thick enough to coat the back of a metal spoon. Immediately remove from the heat.

Nest a mixing bowl in a bowl of ice. Strain the custard through a fine-mesh sieve into the bowl nested in the ice bath. Stir the mixture frequently with the spatula to speed the cooling process.

When the custard is well chilled, transfer it to an ice cream maker and freeze according to the manufacturer's directions. The ice cream is ready when it is the consistency of soft-serve ice cream. If it processes too long, it will become grainy.

Transfer to an airtight container and store in the freezer until ready to use. It will keep for about 1 week.

Strawberry Ice Cream

Makes about 4 cups

1 ¼ cups sugar

———

8 large egg yolks

———

2 pints strawberries, hulled and chopped

———

2 cups plus 1 tablespoon whole milk

———

Place the sugar in a large mixing bowl. Whisk in the egg yolks, beating until well combined and the mixture is thick and smooth.

In a heavy-bottomed saucepan, combine the strawberries and milk. Place over medium-high heat and bring to a boil, stirring occasionally. Immediately remove from the heat.

Slowly pour about one-third of the hot milk mixture into the egg yolk mixture, whisking constantly to temper the yolks. Pour the tempered egg mixture into the remaining hot milk mixture and, stirring constantly with a heatproof rubber spatula, place over medium heat. It should immediately begin to thicken. Cook for about 5 minutes, or until the mixture reaches 182°F on an instant-read thermometer and is thick enough to coat the back of a metal spoon. Immediately remove from the heat.

Nest a mixing bowl in a bowl of ice. Pour the custard into the bowl nested in the ice bath. Stir the mixture frequently with the spatula to speed the cooling process.

When the custard is well chilled, transfer it to a blender or to a food processor fitted with the metal blade and process to a smooth purée. Pour the purée into an ice cream maker and freeze according to the manufacturer's directions. The ice cream is ready when it is the consistency of soft-serve ice cream. If it processes too long, it will become grainy.

Transfer to an airtight container and store in the freezer until ready to use. It will keep for 1 week.

Chocolate Ice Cream

Makes about 4 cups

1 ½ *cups sugar*

8 *large egg yolks*

4 *cups whole milk*

7 *ounces bittersweet chocolate,*
finely chopped

Place the sugar in a large bowl. Whisk in the egg yolks, beating until well combined and the mixture is thick and smooth.

In a heavy-bottomed saucepan, combine the milk and chocolate. Place over medium-high heat and bring to a boil, stirring occasionally. Immediately remove from the heat.

Slowly pour about one-third of the hot milk mixture into the egg yolk mixture, whisking constantly to temper the yolks. Pour the tempered egg mixture into the remaining hot milk mixture and, stirring constantly with a heatproof rubber spatula, place over medium heat. It should immediately begin to thicken. Cook for about 5 minutes, or until the mixture reaches 182°F on an instant-read thermometer and is thick enough to coat the back of a metal spoon. Immediately remove from the heat.

Nest a mixing bowl in a bowl of ice. Pour the custard into the bowl nested in the ice bath. Stir the mixture frequently with a spatula to speed the cooling process.

When the custard is well chilled, transfer it to a blender or to a food processor fitted with the metal blade and process to a smooth purée. Pour the purée into an ice cream maker and freeze according to the manufacturer's directions. The ice cream is ready when it is the consistency of soft-serve ice cream. If it processes too long, it will become grainy.

Transfer to an airtight container and store in the freezer until ready to use. It will keep for 1 week.

Chocolate Cupcakes

Makes 2 dozen cupcales

Who doesn't love a cupcake? Just enough cake to satisfy a sweet tooth, but small enough to be eaten with relatively little guilt, they are a delicious summer indulgence. I like them because both the cupcakes and the buttercream can be made in advance, frozen, and then thawed and iced at the last minute for unexpected guests or spur-of-the-moment parties. If you like, add food coloring to some of the buttercream and garnish the iced cupcakes with piped rosettes or flowers.

3 ½ ounces unsweetened chocolate, chopped

2 tablespoons Dutch-processed cocoa powder

1 ¼ cups boiling water

2 cups cake flour, sifted

¾ teaspoon baking soda

½ teaspoon baking powder

¼ teaspoon salt

1 cup (2 sticks) unsalted butter

1 ½ cups light brown sugar

3 large eggs, at room temperature

½ cup sour cream

2 teaspoons pure vanilla extract

Vanilla Buttercream (recipe follows)

Combine the chocolate and cocoa powder in a heatproof bowl. Add the boiling water and whisk until smooth. Set aside to cool to room temperature.

Preheat the oven to 350°F. Line two 12-cup muffin tins with paper liners.

In a bowl, sift together the flour, baking soda, baking powder, and salt. Set aside.

In the bowl of a stand mixer fitted with the paddle, beat the butter on medium speed for about 3 minutes, or until very light and fluffy. Add the brown sugar and continue to beat until well incorporated. Add the eggs one at a time, beating after each addition until well incorporated.

Reduce the speed to low and beat in the sour cream and vanilla until well blended. Add the flour mixture and beat just until combined.

Scoop an equal amount of the batter into each lined muffin cup, filling the cups about two-thirds full. Bake for about 20 minutes, or until a cake tester inserted in the center comes out clean. Remove from the oven, carefully transfer the cupcakes to wire racks, and let cool completely.

If you wish to freeze them, place them in the freezer on a baking sheet in a single layer. Once frozen, which should take about 1½ hours, transfer to resealable plastic bags, label, and date. Freeze for up to 1 month. Thaw, at room temperature, before using or icing. Spoon the buttercream into a pastry bag fitted with the small star tip and pipe it in a decorative pattern on top of each cupcake.

Vanilla Buttercream

Makes about 3½ cups

¾ cup sugar

———

¼ cup water

———

4 large egg whites, at room temperature

———

1 ½ cups (3 sticks) plus 3 tablespoons unsalted butter, at room temperature, cubed

———

Pure vanilla extract to taste (no more than 2 teaspoons)

———

In a small, heavy-bottomed saucepan, combine the sugar and water. Clip a thermometer to the side of the pan, place over medium-high heat, and heat, without stirring, to 245°F.

When the sugar syrup reaches 245°F, place the egg whites in the bowl of a stand mixer fitted with the whip and beat on high speed until light and fluffy, adjusting the speed if necessary so that the whites are not overbeaten before the syrup is ready.

When the sugar syrup has reached 250°F, remove it from the heat. With the mixer on low speed, carefully pour the hot syrup between the whip and the side of the bowl, taking care not to hit the whip as you pour, or the hot syrup will spatter and burn you. Raise the speed to medium-high and continue beating for about 5 minutes, or until the outside of the bowl is warm but not hot and the mixture is slightly cool.

Raise the speed to high, add the butter all at once, and whip for about 3 minutes, or until thick, smooth, shiny, and well emulsified. Be careful not to overbeat, or the buttercream will become grainy. Beat in the vanilla.

Use immediately, or cover tightly and store in the refrigerator for up to 3 days, or freeze in an airtight container for up to 2 months and thaw before using. When ready to use, whip again to soften to spreading consistency.

Chocolate Almond Cake

Makes 1 loaf

J'm not sure if I should call this dessert confection or cake. Rich, dark, and entirely flourless, it is a very elegant dessert that can be served as is, or extravagantly sauced with a raspberry purée or crème anglaise (page 106) and then decorated with whipped cream or a chocolate treat. Served nice and chilled, it's just perfect for a hot summer's night, as you never even have to turn on the oven. It will keep, tightly wrapped and refrigerated, for at least a week.

15 ounces bittersweet chocolate, finely chopped

4 tablespoons unsalted butter, at room temperature

1 cup heavy cream, at room temperature

4 large egg yolks, at room temperature

1 cup confectioners' sugar, sifted

3 tablespoons almond liqueur

1 cup slivered blanched almonds, toasted, plus more for garnish, optional

Whipped cream for garnish, optional

Mint sprigs or Chocolate Fans (page 37), optional

Lightly oil a 3-cup loaf pan, decorative mold, or terrine. If using a loaf pan or terrine, cut a piece of parchment paper to fit the length of the pan, leaving about 2 inches hanging over each end. Fit the parchment into the pan. Cut another piece of parchment to fit the bottom and width of the pan, leaving about 2 inches hanging over each side. Carefully fit the parchment into the pan. The bottom and all sides should now be completely covered with parchment. If using a decorative mold, lightly butter the entire interior.

Place the chocolate and butter in the top half of a double boiler. Place over (not touching) gently simmering water in the bottom pan and heat, stirring frequently, just until the chocolate begins to melt and the butter is blending into it. Add the cream while whisking constantly. Cook, stirring constantly, for about 5 minutes, or until the mixture has blended completely.

Warm a large bowl (a quick spin in the microwave will do it easily). In a small bowl, whisk the egg yolks just to loosen. Whisk in a bit of the warm chocolate mixture to temper the yolks.

Pour the remaining chocolate mixture into the warmed bowl and whisk in the tempered egg yolks. Add the confectioners' sugar and continue to whisk until completely blended, very smooth, and shiny. Stir in the liqueur and almonds.

Scrape the chocolate mixture into the prepared pan. Using an offset spatula, carefully smooth the top. Lightly cover the top with plastic film, and place the pan in the refrigerator. Refrigerate for at least 8 hours, or until quite firm, or for up to 1 week.

When ready to serve, invert the mold or lift the loaf from the pan by pulling on the overhanging parchment paper (if the cake doesn't fall out, wrap a hot towel around the mold for a few seconds and it should pop right out). Invert the loaf onto a cutting board and carefully peel off the parchment.

Using a sharp knife or a wire cheese cutter, cut the molded cake into small wedges, or cut the loaf into slices about ¼ inch thick. Place 2 slices or wedges, slightly overlapping, on each dessert plate. Place a dollop of whipped cream in the center, sprinkle with toasted almonds, and garnish with a mint sprig or Chocolate Fan. Serve chilled.

Chocolate-Covered Cereal

Makes about 6 dozen

This is an easy-to-make, kid-friendly treat, especially in the summer when no cook wants to heat up the kitchen. I first made this with cornflakes, but have since used many other types of non-sugar-coated cereals, like Cheerios and Rice Krispies. This can even be a great, slightly indulgent breakfast treat, for kids and adults alike.

4 cups very crisp cornflakes or other non-sugar-coated flaked cereal

1 pound bittersweet chocolate, tempered (page 13)

Line 2 rimmed baking sheets with parchment paper.

Place the cereal in a large bowl. Pour about half of the chocolate over the cereal and, using a rubber spatula, toss the cereal around to coat evenly. The chocolate will begin to set. When the first coating has set, pour in the remaining chocolate and again toss to coat evenly.

Working quickly while the chocolate is still pliable, scoop up small mounds of the the cereal and place them on the prepared baking sheets. Set aside for about 30 minutes, or until hardened completely. If your kitchen is very hot, you can place the baking sheets in the refrigerator for no more than 10 minutes to speed the setting.

Layer the cereal clusters, separated by sheets of waxed paper, in an airtight container and store at room temperature for up to 2 weeks.

Chocolate Lollipops

Makes 20 to 30 pops

This is such an easy recipe—great to make with kids during the summer months when they're off from school and itching to stay busy. You can use commercial lollipop molds (Sources, page 192), or you can make your own as I do. Since the homemade molds are made with Play-Doh modeling clay, even children can help make them. They are always so proud to have made their very own candy. I have given three different types of chocolate here, but you can use only one type if you like. The white chocolate can also be tinted with food coloring.

1 pound bittersweet chocolate, tempered (page 13)

———

1 pound milk chocolate, tempered (page 13)

———

1 pound white chocolate, tempered (page 13)

———

Pour the tempered chocolate directly into the plastic lollipop molds, filling to the top. Lightly tap the molds against the work surface to release any air bubbles in the chocolate.

Set the lollipop sticks in place by inserting them just far enough to be firmly placed in the chocolate in the mold. Set aside for about 30 minutes to allow the chocolate to set.

When set, simply pop the lollipops out of their molds and eat.

SEPTEMBER & OCTOBER

End of Summer, Back to School, and Halloween

The end of summer is greeted with glee at Jacques Torres Chocolate: hot, humid, unkind-to-chocolate days slowly evolve into crisp autumn ones that herald no more "hot" chocolate worries. It is also a time of intense preparation, as we get ready for the busy days ahead that begin with Halloween's trick-or-treat candies and end with fat Santas and sugarplums dancing in our heads.

Back-to-school days have mothers stockpiling chocolate treats for lunch boxes, and weekends find our stores filled with kids, delighted to have free time to explore a chocolate factory. We often have demonstrations in the store on Saturday mornings, with visiting children as active participants. The kids have no inhibitions and love to advise and assist me as I work, which makes these events especially enjoyable. They seem to believe that I couldn't possibly mold chocolate without their help, and their self-confidence almost convinces me that I couldn't.

Halloween is celebrated in the United States with great intensity. I love seeing the children dressed up and out-and-about, with some of them just on the edge of terror, and others thrilled at the idea of frightening the wits out of everyone else. They have no idea that we can see right through their costumes.

I also love the creative costumes. In New York, people, mostly adults, dress up to the extreme. The big parade through Greenwich Village, which begins near our factory, is over-the-top with nearly unbelievable ensembles.

Peanut Butter Cups

———

Chocolate Caramel Corn

———

Brittle with Pumpkin Seeds and Cranberries

———

Filled Chocolate Cookies

———

All-Occasion Chocolate Cake

———

Chocolate Dippers

———

Cream-Filled Chocolate Doughnuts

Men dressed as women, women dressed as men, and both dressed in outfits that stretch the boundaries of imagination. Outer space has nothing on New York on All Hallow's Eve!

I take a few moments during this month to carve my pumpkins out of chocolate, sometimes using colored cocoa butter to make them look as though they have come straight from the farm. Rather than the traditional candy-coated apples, I sometimes cover crisp, just-harvested apples with chocolate. Chocolate Caramel Corn (page 136) is one of our favorite Halloween treats, so I always make a big batch. In the stores, we always have small chocolate pumpkins and lollipops in the shape of witches, bats, pumpkins, and ghosts for giving to trick-or-treaters who stop by.

Peanut Butter Cups

Makes 16 minicups

You can make these great back-to-school treats in any size you want and with as much décor as your patience and creativity allow. In this recipe I suggest using foil or paper candy cups or miniature cupcake liners, but you can also use nonstick mini-muffin pans or small tart tins to mold the cups. The smaller sizes are terrific treats for kids, while the larger ones are good desserts for grown-ups.

Peanut butter is an American phenomenon. I had never tasted it until I came to the States, but unlike many of my compatriots, I have become an enthusiastic convert. Now I even make my own to use in bonbon and bar fillings.

12 ounces bittersweet chocolate, tempered (page 13)

5 ounces bittersweet chocolate, finely chopped

1 cup (about 9 ounces) smooth peanut butter

Place 2 sheets of parchment paper on a clean, flat work surface. Place 1 or 2 wire racks on the parchment.

Place the tempered chocolate in a warmed bowl. Using a small, soft brush and working with 1 cup at a time, lightly coat the interior of 16 fluted paper or foil cups measuring about 1 inch in diameter and ¾ inch high with a thin coat of the tempered chocolate, taking care that the paper is evenly coated. As the cups are coated, set them on the racks and let stand for about 5 minutes to set.

When all of the cups have been coated, repeat the process one more time and return them to the racks. When the second coat has been applied, place the cups in the refrigerator for about 10 minutes to harden completely.

Meanwhile, place the chopped chocolate in the top half of a double boiler. Place over (not touching) gently simmering water in the bottom pan and heat, stirring occasionally, for about 4 minutes, or until completely melted. Remove the chocolate from the heat and continue stirring to cool slightly. When cool enough to touch easily, beat in the peanut butter. The chocolate must not be too hot, or it will cause the oil in the peanut butter to separate out.

Scrape the peanut butter mixture into a pastry bag fitted with medium-sized plain tip. Remove the cups from the refrigerator and begin piping an equal portion of the peanut butter mixture into each cup, stopping within about ⅛ inch of the rim. If desired, smooth the top of each cup with a small offset spatula. Let stand for about 1 hour, or until the filling is set. If your kitchen is warm, return the filled cups to the refrigerator for about 15 minutes to set completely. Store, airtight, in a cool spot for up to 3 days.

Chocolate Caramel Corn

Makes about 10 cups

ℐ didn't know that Halloween was such a big holiday until I came to the States. Now, I'm the first to put on a costume and engage in holiday mischief! This sweet, crunchy confection is addictively good, perfect for a trick-or-treat bag. Kids and their parents love it. I like to use bittersweet chocolate, but you can use any type or combination you prefer.

Be extremely careful when working with caramel, as it can burn terribly. Have a big bowl of ice water nearby, so that if you are spattered with hot caramel, you can quickly immerse your hands or arms into the soothing cold.

1 cup popping corn

1 cup sugar

⅓ cup light corn syrup

½ cup (1 stick) plus 2 tablespoons unsalted butter

½ teaspoon salt

1 teaspoon baking soda

1 pound bittersweet, milk, or white chocolate, tempered (page 13)

Line a large baking pan with parchment paper. Set aside.

Pop the corn by your usual method, but use no oil and add no salt. Set aside.

Combine the sugar, corn syrup, butter, and salt in a heavy-bottomed saucepan large enough to hold the popped corn. Clip a thermometer to the side of the pan, place the pan over medium-high heat, and heat, without stirring, until the mixture registers 311°F. Stir in the baking soda, taking care, as it will cause the mixture to bubble up. Then quickly add the popcorn and stir rapidly with a wooden spoon to coat the corn evenly with the caramel. Scrape the caramel corn onto the prepared baking pan, pushing it out evenly over the bottom of the pan to avoid clumping. Let cool completely. Once cool, break up any clumps with your hands.

Transfer the caramel corn to a large bowl. Gradually ladle the chocolate over the caramel corn while stirring with a wooden spoon to coat evenly. Continue stirring until all of the corn is nicely covered. Let cool completely.

Serve immediately, or store, tightly covered, in a cool spot for a day or two.

Brittle with Pumpkin Seeds and Cranberries

Makes about 4 pounds

The flavors of this candy are awesome—the sweet brittle absolutely pops with the tartness of the cranberries mellowed by the delicate pepitas. Reminiscent of Mexico, where pumpkin seeds make their way into all types of dishes, the chocolate coating seals the Latin touch. Broken into pieces and attractively packed in a tin, this candy makes a perfect hostess gift.

Always take extra care when making brittle because hot caramel burns badly. Have a big bowl of ice water nearby, so that if you are spattered with hot caramel, you can quickly immerse your hands or arms into the soothing cold.

1½ cups (3 sticks) unsalted butter

———

1¾ cups granulated sugar

———

1 cup light corn syrup

———

2 teaspoons salt

———

1 teaspoon baking soda

———

2 teaspoons pure vanilla extract

———

10 ounces hulled pumpkin seeds, toasted

———

5 ounces dried cranberries

———

6 ounces bittersweet chocolate, tempered (page 13)

———

Lightly oil two 15½-inch-long jelly roll pans or a clean, flat work surface, preferably of marble or another cool material.

Place the butter in a large heavy-bottomed saucepan over medium heat. When melted, stir in the sugar and corn syrup and raise the heat to high. Clip a thermometer to the side of the pan and cook, stirring constantly, for about 4 minutes, or until the mixture comes to a boil. Continue to boil, stirring constantly, for about 15 minutes, or until the mixture is golden brown and registers 315°F on the thermometer.

Remove from the heat and stir in the salt and baking soda, taking care, as the soda will cause the mixture to boil up. Stir in the vanilla. Add the pumpkin seeds and cranberries, stirring to thoroughly blend.

Pour an equal amount of the hot mixture into each oiled pan (or onto the oiled surface), spreading it out to about ¼ inch thick with an offset spatula.

When the brittle has set, use a sharp chef's knife to crack it into individual pieces.

Place one or two wire racks on parchment paper.

Place the tempered chocolate in a warmed bowl and, using tongs, dip each piece of brittle into the chocolate, lifting it up to allow the excess chocolate to drip off. Place the chocolate-dipped brittle on the wire racks to set. You may have to dip a couple of times to completely cover the candy. You may also dip only half of each piece. If so, dip on the bias for a more attractive pattern. Let stand for about 30 minutes, or until the chocolate has hardened completely.

Serve immediately or store layered in an airtight container, for up to 1 week.

Filled Chocolate Cookies

Makes about 3 dozen cookies

A fancier version of everyday chocolate sandwich cookies, these buttery gems, which conceal a rich mocha filling, require a cookie press for their elegant shape. If you don't have one, roll out the dough ⅛ inch thick on a lightly floured work surface and cut out 1 ½- to 2-inch circles with a cookie cutter or biscuit cutter. Bake and fill as directed in the recipe.

1 cup (2 sticks) unsalted butter, at room temperature

3 ounces cream cheese, at room temperature

1 cup sugar

1 large egg

2 ounces unsweetened chocolate, melted and cooled to room temperature

1 teaspoon pure vanilla extract

2½ cups all-purpose flour

1 teaspoon baking powder

Mocha Filling (recipe follows)

Place the butter and cream cheese in the bowl of a stand mixer fitted with the paddle. Beat on low speed to just combine. Add the sugar and beat on medium speed for about 3 minutes or until light and fluffy. Add the egg and beat to incorporate. Add the chocolate and vanilla and beat to blend.

Sift the flour and baking powder together. Lower the mixer speed and slowly beat in the flour mixture to make a firm dough.

Lay a piece of plastic film on a clean, flat work surface. Using a rubber spatula, scrape the dough from the mixer bowl. Pat into a large disk and wrap it in the plastic film. Place in the refrigerator for at least 30 minutes or up to 3 days. If refrigerated for a longer period, it may get quite firm. In this case, just let it sit at room temperature for a while to become more pliable.

Preheat the oven to 350°F.

Line 2 cookie sheets with parchment paper.

Fill a cookie press fitted with the star plate with the dough. Press stars out on the parchment-lined cookie sheets, spacing them about ½ inch apart. The dough may also be pressed into cookie molds.

Bake for about 10 minutes, or until just barely brown around the edges. Remove from the oven and let rest for 5 minutes. Then transfer to wire racks to cool.

When cool, turn half of the cookies flat side up. Working with one cookie at a time, spread an equal portion of the Mocha Filling over each flat side. Cover the filling with another cookie, flat side facing the filling. Set aside for about 30 minutes, or until the filling has set.

Serve or store, layered in an airtight container, for up to 3 days.

Mocha Filling

6 ounces bittersweet chocolate, finely chopped

―――

2 teaspoons espresso coffee powder

―――

½ cup heavy cream

―――

½ cup (1 stick) unsalted butter, at room temperature

―――

2 cups sifted confectioners' sugar

―――

Combine the chocolate and coffee powder in a medium mixing bowl. Set aside.

Place the cream in a heavy-bottomed saucepan over medium heat. Bring to just a bare simmer. Immediately remove from the heat and, using a wooden spoon, beat the hot cream into the chocolate mixture. As soon as the chocolate begins to melt, beat in the butter. When the butter has melted and the mixture is well blended, begin beating in the confectioners' sugar.

When smooth and homogenous, use as directed in the recipe. If not using immediately, cover with plastic film and keep at room temperature until ready to use.

All-Occasion Chocolate Cake

Makes one 2-layer, 8-inch cake

This cake is simple to make, assemble, and decorate. The base is a classic French genoise, which can be baked up to 3 weeks in advance and frozen until you need it. The ganache frosting is everyone's favorite, and can be used for countless other cakes. As for the décor, you can either assemble and frost the cake and say "let's eat," or you can decorate the top with piped ganache, fresh fruit or flowers, or any flourish appropriate to the occasion.

Chocolate genoise can also be made with butter. Simply substitute 5 ½ tablespoons cooled, melted unsalted butter for the 3 egg yolks, and fold it into the batter after the flour mixture has been incorporated.

8 large whole eggs

3 large egg yolks

1 cup sugar

2 ½ tablespoons honey

2 cups sifted cake flour

⅓ cup Dutch-processed cocoa powder

Chocolate Ganache Frosting (recipe follows)

Preheat the oven to 375°F. Lightly butter two 8-inch round cake pans. Line the bottoms with parchment paper and lightly butter the parchment.

In a large heatproof bowl, combine the whole eggs, egg yolks, sugar, and honey. Select a 1-quart saucepan in which the bowl will fit snugly in the rim. Fill the pan halfway with water, place over medium heat, and bring the water to a simmer. Place the bowl over (not touching) the simmering water and whisk for about 10 minutes, or until very foamy and the mixture registers 113°F. When the mixture is ready, it should be hot to the touch, tripled in volume, and fall back into the bowl in a thick ribbon when the whisk is lifted.

Remove the bowl from the heat and transfer the mixture to the bowl of a stand mixer fitted with the whip. Beat on medium-high speed for about 10 minutes, or until the mixture has cooled and further increased in volume. It should be pale yellow and slightly stiff.

Remove the bowl from the mixer. Combine the flour and cocoa powder in a sifter or fine-mesh sieve. Slowly sift the flour mixture onto the egg mixture, folding it in with a rubber spatula at the same time. Be sure to reach to the bottom of the bowl to ensure a completely mixed batter. Do not beat or overfold, or the batter will deflate and the cake will be dense.

Carefully transfer an equal portion of the batter to each prepared pan. Bake for about 30 minutes, or until lightly colored and springy to the touch. Remove from the oven and let cool in the pans on wire racks for about 10 minutes. Then invert the cakes onto the racks, lift off the pans, and let cool completely. Peel off the parchment paper. (The cakes may be made up to this point, tightly wrapped in plastic film, and frozen for up to 3 weeks.)

When ready to assemble, place 1 of the cakes on a cake plate. Using an offset spatula, cover the top with about ⅓ cup of the frosting. Place the second cake on top and, using the spatula, carefully cover the top and the sides of the cake completely with the remaining frosting. Serve immediately, or store, covered and refrigerated, for up to 2 days.

Chocolate Ganache Frosting

Makes about 4 cups

21 ounces bittersweet chocolate, finely chopped

2 ¼ cups heavy cream

¼ cup Grand Marnier or any other liqueur of choice

Place the chocolate in a heatproof bowl. Make sure it is finely chopped so it will melt quickly. Place the cream in a heavy-bottomed saucepan over medium heat and heat just until distinct bubbles begin to form around the edges of the pan. Remove from the heat, slowly pour about half of the hot cream over the chocolate, and let stand for 30 seconds, until the chocolate begins to melt. Using an immersion blender, begin beating the cream into the melting chocolate. As the cream and chocolate emulsify, slowly add the remaining hot cream, continuing to beat with the blender. Add the liqueur and beat to incorporate.

Cover the bowl with plastic film and set aside to rest until the ganache has cooled and is velvety smooth, shiny, and thick (it should be about the consistency of toothpaste). It will keep, covered and refrigerated, for up to 1 week. Bring to room temperature and beat to a spreadable consistency before using.

NOTE: If the ganache separates (collapses and liquefies) while you are incorporating the hot cream, it is easy to fix. Beat in a small amount of cold heavy cream before adding the liqueur (or any other flavoring).

Chocolate Dippers

Makes about 4 dozen

Full of crunch and character, these milk chocolate–almond cookies are not your typical after-school snack, but they'll soon become your favorite. They're delicious dipped in a glass of milk or a cup of hot coffee. They keep well and are great to keep on hand for afternoon snacking.

⅔ cup chopped almonds

3 ½ ounces milk chocolate, chopped

Scant 1 cup all-purpose flour

½ cup sugar

⅓ cup plus 2 teaspoons Dutch-processed cocoa powder

Pinch of salt

2 large eggs, at room temperature

1 teaspoon pure vanilla extract

1 large egg white, lightly beaten

Preheat the oven to 300°F. Line a rimmed baking sheet with parchment paper, and spread the almonds on the parchment in a single layer. Place in the oven and toast for about 30 minutes, or until golden brown. Remove from the oven and let cool completely on the pan on a wire rack.

Combine the milk chocolate and flour in the bowl of a food processor fitted with the metal blade and pulse with quick on-off bursts until a coarse flour forms.

Transfer the chocolate "flour" to a stand mixer fitted with the paddle and add the sugar, cocoa powder, and salt, stirring to blend. Add the eggs and vanilla and beat on medium speed for about 5 minutes, or until well combined and a soft dough forms. Remove the bowl from the mixer and fold in the toasted almonds with a rubber spatula.

Cover the bowl with plastic film and refrigerate for about 1 hour, or until the dough is firm enough to shape.

Preheat the oven to 350°F. Line 2 cookie sheets with parchment paper.

Lightly flour a clean, flat work surface. Divide the dough into 3 equal pieces. Place 1 piece of the dough on the floured work surface and, using your palms, roll the dough into a rope the length of a cookie sheet and 1 to 1 ½ inches in diameter. Roll it firmly to remove any air bubbles. If your hands get sticky, lightly dust them with flour. (The dough may be made up to this point, tightly wrapped, and frozen for up to 2 weeks. Thaw at room temperature before proceeding with the recipe.) Repeat with the remaining 2 dough pieces.

Place 2 ropes on 1 prepared cookie sheet, leaving a good amount of space between them to allow the dough to spread. Place the remaining rope on the other prepared cookie sheet. Using a pastry brush, lightly coat each rope with the egg white.

Bake for about 30 minutes, or until light brown. Remove from the oven and let cool slightly on the pans on wire racks.

When still quite warm yet cool enough to handle, transfer to a cutting board and using a serrated knife, cut each rope crosswise on the diagonal into ½-inch-thick pieces. Place the pieces on wire racks and let cool completely. If the dough cools too much, the pieces will crumble when cut, so you must work quickly. If the dough seems too soft when cut, return the sliced cookies to a 300°F oven and bake for an additional 10 to 15 minutes, or until cooked through and crisp.

Serve immediately, or store in an airtight container at room temperature for up to 1 week.

Cream-Filled Chocolate Doughnuts

Makes about 2 dozen

Warm, puffy doughnuts were just meant to be eaten on crisp autumn days. These doughnuts, made of rich chocolate brioche dough fried up into airy, warm rounds and filled with thick, cool pastry cream, are particularly special. Kids love them: The crunchy sugar coating and the oozing cream on little fingers makes for yummy licking. Adults don't mind them either!

3 ½ cups all-purpose flour

1 ⅔ cups high-gluten flour

¾ cup plus 2 tablespoons Dutch-processed cocoa powder

3 ½ cups sugar

4 teaspoons salt

3 envelopes (2 ½ teaspoons each) active dry yeast

7 large eggs, at room temperature

About 1 cup water

1 ¾ cups (3 ½ sticks) unsalted butter, cut into small pieces, chilled

6 cups vegetable oil for deep-frying

Pastry Cream (recipe follows)

Lightly flour a nonstick baking sheet.

In the bowl of a stand mixer fitted with the dough hook, combine the flours, cocoa powder, 1 ½ cups of the sugar, and the salt. Add the yeast. Mix on low speed just until the ingredients are evenly distributed. Add the eggs and continue to mix while slowly adding the water. Because different flours absorb liquid at different rates, depending on the amount of natural moisture in the flour, the humidity of the kitchen, and so on, you won't always need all the water. You want a dough that holds together, is well blended, and is not too wet or sticky, so if it has reached that point before you have added all of the water, don't add the rest of it.

Add all of the butter pieces and beat on medium speed for 4 to 5 minutes, or until the butter is completely incorporated into the dough. At this point, the dough should be smooth and elastic, yet slightly sticky to the touch.

Turn the dough out onto the floured baking sheet and pat it into a round. Cover with plastic film and let the dough rise in a warm place for 1 hour, or until doubled in bulk.

Lightly flour 2 rimmed baking sheets. Uncover the dough and remove it from the baking sheet. Divide the dough into 24 equal pieces. (Each piece should weigh about 4 ounces.) Using your hands, form each piece into a 2-inch round. As the rounds are shaped, place them on the prepared baking sheets, spacing them about 3 inches apart.

Cover the baking sheets with plastic film and let the rounds rise in a warm place for 1 hour, or until doubled in volume.

Line a large tray with a triple thickness of paper towels. Place the remaining 2 cups sugar in a resealable plastic bag or deep bowl. Pour the oil into a deep-fryer or a heavy-bottomed saucepan with a basket insert and heat to 320°F.

Place the basket in the hot oil and add a few dough rounds to it. Fry, turning once with a slotted spoon or spider, for about 4 minutes, or until puffed and lightly colored. Using the slotted spoon, transfer the doughnuts to the paper towels to drain. Repeat with the remaining dough rounds.

When the doughnuts are drained but still warm, add them to the bag of sugar and shake or toss to coat well on all sides.

Spoon the Pastry Cream into a pastry bag fitted with a small plain tip. Working with one doughnut at a time, poke the tip into the side and gently force a squeeze of cream into the interior of the doughnut. Serve warm.

Pastry Cream

Makes about 2 ½ cups

½ cup plus 2 tablespoons sugar

2 tablespoons plus 1 teaspoon cornstarch

2 large whole eggs

2 large egg yolks

2 cups plus 1 tablespoon whole milk

1 vanilla bean, split in half lengthwise

3½ tablespoons unsalted butter, at room temperature, cut into tiny pieces, optional

Sift together half of the sugar and the cornstarch into a bowl. Whisk in the whole eggs and egg yolks until well blended, thick, and smooth. Set aside.

In a heavy-bottomed nonreactive saucepan, combine the milk with the remaining sugar. Using the edge of a small, sharp knife, scrape the seeds from the vanilla bean into the milk and then add the bean. Place over medium heat and bring to a boil, whisking occasionally. Remove from the heat.

Whisking constantly, whisk about one-third of the hot milk mixture into the egg mixture. Pour this mixture into the remaining hot milk, whisk to combine, and return to medium-low heat. Cook, whisking constantly to keep the mixture from sticking and burning. Just before the mixture comes to a boil, it should thicken enough to coat the back of a spoon. As soon as the mixture boils, lower the heat slightly and continue to whisk for another 2 minutes to cook out the raw taste of the cornstarch and to allow the flavors to mellow.

Remove from the heat and strain through a fine-mesh sieve into a clean bowl. Using a rubber spatula, fold in the butter a little at a time. (The butter gives the cream a little sheen.)

Cover with plastic film, pressing it directly on the surface to keep a skin from forming, and let cool to room temperature. If not using immediately, cover tightly and refrigerate for up to 3 days.

NOVEMBER

Day of the Dead and Thanksgiving

When I began researching chocolate, I immediately became fascinated with its connection to the history of Mexico. One of the first excursions I made in my quest for chocolate lore was to the city of Oaxaca for the Day of the Dead (*Día de los Muertos*) celebration, a thrilling spectacle that pays homage to death in unique ways. A skeletal figure called La Catrina (as well as many other names) is the symbol of the holiday, a cultural phenomenon unlike anything I had ever experienced and one in which chocolate plays a big role. To this day, Oaxaca remains a spellbinding destination that I hope to return to often.

Preparation for Day of the Dead revelries begins in mid-October when markets jump-start the excitement by stocking all of the required regalia. There are brilliantly colored tissue-paper cutouts called *papel picado*, skeletons in every form and guise, demonic toys, paper and papier-mâché religious artifacts, decorative wreaths, and incense. You'll also find fresh flowers, particularly marigolds and cockscomb, for sale everywhere, along with votives and other candles that will be used to light the way to the cemeteries and to illuminate graves and crypts.

Throughout most of Mexico, the Day of the Dead celebrations are held on November 1, All Saints' Day, and on November 2, All Souls' Day, with traditional practices specific to each region. But common to all of the areas are the festive family reunions at ancestral burial plots. Special foods are prepared and left for the departed on handmade altars at the gravesides. In most communities, deceased children (*angelitos*) are honored on November 1, and departed adults are remembered on November 2.

The edible offerings prepared during this period include candies made from chocolate, sugar, and seeds and shaped into macabre shapes, such as skulls, skeletons, and coffins, and sweet breads and rolls often topped with skeleton or bone shapes fashioned from dough. Other doughs are formed into Frankenstein-like creatures called *animas*, which represent the souls of the departed. All of these are placed on the grave as offerings to the dead, along with tequila, beer, *atole* (a thick, corn-based beverage), chocolate beverages, or even fresh water to drink and plenty of hearty foods, such as rice and beans, vegetables and potatoes, and meats in mole sauces, to satisfy their hunger. A similar repast might also be placed on a home altar to make sure that the departed souls feel welcome should they wish to make a home visit. It is an extraordinary experience—even New York's uproarious Greenwich Village Halloween celebration pales in comparison!

I've never quite had the daring to go full-out and mimic the ghoulish Mexican candies in chocolate. Our Halloween witches and ghosts are the nearest I get to them. However, I always try to celebrate the Day of the Dead with a Mexican dinner based on some kind of mole. I love the idea that chocolate has in its heritage this deliciously savory sauce, so far from the bonbons and bars of our daily life.

Our Day of the Dead celebration is but a blip on our fall season, as pumpkins quickly give way to trays of turkeys, overflowing cornucopias, footballs, and other chocolate mementos of our day of thanks. Although football seems to be the most popular Thanksgiving pastime, chocolate turkeys are the biggest sellers in the stores. By the time Thanksgiving Day rolls around, we all find it difficult to enjoy the real thing!

Pumpkin Chocolate Cake

———

Soft Chocolate Caramels

———

Chocolate Chocolate Biscotti

———

European Peanut Butter Chocolates

———

Chocolate Tuiles

———

Chocolate Almond Chews

———

Chocolate Babka

———

Pain au Chocolat

Pumpkin Chocolate Cake

Makes one 8-inch Bundt cake

Rich with the flavors of fall and winter, this sensational snacking cake is aromatic with spices, moist with mellow pumpkin, and studded with chocolate, cranberries, and nuts. Easy to make for the holiday season when lots of entertaining is on the agenda, it is also a terrific keeper (refrigerated or frozen) for last-minute get-togethers. For an even deeper chocolate flavor, substitute ¼ cup Dutch-processed cocoa for ¼ cup of the flour.

½ cup (1 stick) plus 1 tablespoon unsalted butter

¾ cup light brown sugar

2 large eggs, at room temperature

1 cup canned pumpkin purée

1 ¼ cups cake flour

1 teaspoon baking soda

1 teaspoon ground cinnamon

½ teaspoon grated nutmeg

¼ teaspoon ground cloves

¼ teaspoon salt

3 ounces (½ cup) chopped 60% bittersweet chocolate

½ cup dried cranberries

½ cup chopped walnuts

2 tablespoons confectioners' sugar, optional

1 tablespoon Dutch-processed cocoa powder, optional

Chocolate Glaze (recipe follows), optional

Preheat the oven to 350°F.

Lightly butter and flour a 6-cup bundt pan. Set aside.

Place the butter in the bowl of an electric mixer fitted with the paddle. Beat on medium speed to just soften. Add the brown sugar and beat for about 4 minutes, or until very light and creamy. Reduce the speed to low and add the eggs, one at a time, beating well after each addition. Add the pumpkin and beat to blend.

Combine the flour, baking soda, cinnamon, nutmeg, cloves, and salt and, with the motor off, sift the dry ingredients into the pumpkin mixture. Turn the speed to low and beat to incorporate the dry ingredients into the pumpkin mixture. When well blended, remove the bowl from the mixer and, using a rubber spatula, fold in the chocolate, cranberries, and nuts.

Scrape the batter into the prepared pan. Bake for about 40 minutes, or until a cake tester inserted near the center comes out clean.

Remove from the oven and invert onto a wire rack. Remove the pan and allow the cake to cool to room temperature.

When cool, transfer the cake to a serving plate, placing the decorative side up. Place the confectioners' sugar and cocoa powder in a fine-mesh sieve and, tapping gently on the side of the sieve, lightly dust the cake with the sugar-cocoa mix. Or, for a more elegant cake, omit the dusting and drizzle the cooled cake with Chocolate Glaze. Cut into slices and serve.

The cake will keep, covered and refrigerated, for up to 4 days or frozen for up to 3 months.

Chocolate Glaze

8 ounces bittersweet chocolate, finely chopped

1 cup heavy cream

Place the chocolate in a heatproof bowl. Set aside.

Place the cream in a medium heavy-bottomed saucepan over medium heat and bring to a boil. Immediately remove from the heat and pour over the chocolate. Let rest for a few seconds and then begin incorporating the cream into the chocolate by mixing with a rubber spatula.

When well blended, drizzle over the cooled cake. Let stand for a few minutes to harden slightly before cutting.

Soft Chocolate Caramels

Makes about 19 dozen

These wonderfully soft, chewy caramels are one of my favorite candies, particularly when they are coated in chocolate. They are perfect for gift giving, as they can be made in advance, wrapped in sparkly candy wrappers, and packed in a clear plastic bag or a fancy container.

2 ½ cups sugar

½ cup plus 2 tablespoons light corn syrup

¼ cup water

½ cup (1 stick) unsalted butter

4 cups heavy cream

1 ¾ teaspoons salt

1 ½ teaspoons strained fresh lemon juice

1 vanilla bean, split in half lengthwise

3 ½ tablespoons cocoa butter

1 pound bittersweet chocolate, tempered (page 13)

Line a large rimmed baking sheet (ideally a jelly-roll or half sheet pan about 13 by 18 inches by 1 inch) with plastic film, allowing it to drape over the sides.

In a heavy-bottomed saucepan, combine ½ cup of the sugar and 2 tablespoons of the corn syrup. Clip a thermometer to the side of the pan. Place the pan over medium-high heat and bring to a boil, stirring frequently. Lower the heat to a simmer and cook without stirring for about 10 minutes, until the mixture registers 228°F and is a dark caramel color. Remove from the heat, add the water, and stir to deglaze the pan. This is called a caramel *mou.*

In a large, heavy-bottomed saucepan, combine the remaining 2 cups sugar, the remaining ½ cup corn syrup, the caramel *mou,* 4 tablespoons of the butter, the cream, salt, and lemon juice. Using the edge of a small, sharp knife, scrape the seeds from the vanilla bean into the mixture. Clip the thermometer to the side of the pan, place the pan over medium heat, and bring to a boil, stirring occasionally. Boil until the mixture registers 250°F.

Meanwhile, combine the cocoa butter and the remaining 4 tablespoons butter in a heatproof bowl. When the caramel mixture is ready, remove it from the heat and pour it into the bowl while beating constantly with a wooden spoon. Continue beating until the mixture is smooth and well blended.

Immediately pour the mixture into the prepared baking pan, lightly smoothing the top with a spatula. Set aside to rest for at least 6 hours or up to overnight.

Line a large rimmed baking sheet with parchment paper. Lift the hardened candy from the baking sheet by lifting it up by the plastic overhang. Place on a flat work surface and, using a sharp chef's knife, cut it into 1-inch squares.

Place the tempered chocolate in a warmed bowl. Working with one candy at a time, drop the caramel into the chocolate. Using a dipping fork, lift out the caramel and hold it over the bowl to allow excess chocolate to drip off. Then gently scrape the bottom of the fork against the side of the bowl to remove any excess chocolate from the bottom of the caramel. As the caramels are coated, place them on the prepared baking sheet. Let rest for about 30 minutes, or until the chocolate has hardened.

Wrap each candy in plastic film or a candy wrapper. Store the caramels in an airtight container at room temperature for up to 1 week.

Chocolate Chocolate Biscotti

Makes about 5 ½ dozen cookies

B iscotti are those famous Italian cookies popular for dipping into hot espresso. I've adapted the classic recipe by cramming them with chocolate and baking them only once (biscotti are customarily baked twice for extra-hard crispness) so they're not quite so jaw-breaking. I keep the traditional flavor of anise, which I think works well with chocolate.

⅓ cup shelled pistachios

¼ cup raw almonds

1 ⅓ cups all-purpose flour

¾ cup Dutch-processed cocoa powder

1 teaspoon baking powder

Pinch of salt

¾ cup sugar

7 tablespoons unsalted butter, cubed, chilled

2 large eggs, at room temperature

Freshly grated zest of 1 lemon

1 tablespoon aniseed

1 pound bittersweet chocolate, tempered (page 13)

1 egg white, lightly beaten

Preheat the oven to 300°F. Line a rimmed baking sheet with parchment paper, and spread the pistachios and almonds on the parchment in a single layer. Place in the oven and toast until golden brown. Remove from the oven and let cool completely on the pan on a wire rack.

Raise the oven temperature to 350°F. Line 2 cookie sheets with parchment paper.

In a bowl, stir together the flour, cocoa powder, baking powder, and salt. Set aside. In the bowl of a stand mixer fitted with the paddle, combine the sugar and butter, beating to blend. Add the eggs and beat on medium speed until well incorporated. Stop the mixer and add the flour mixture. Turn on the mixer to medium-high speed and beat for about 3 minutes, or until a soft dough forms. Reduce the speed to low, add the lemon zest, aniseed, and cooled nuts, and beat just until evenly distributed. Do not overbeat, or the nuts will be crushed.

Lightly flour a clean, flat work surface. Using a rubber spatula, scrape the dough onto the floured surface. (If the dough is too sticky to work with, flatten it slightly, wrap in plastic film, and refrigerate for about 1 hour to firm it.) Divide the dough into 3 equal pieces. Using your palms, roll each piece of dough into a rope the length of a cookie sheet and 1 to 1 ½ inches in diameter. Roll it firmly to remove any air bubbles. If your hands get sticky, lightly dust them with flour. Repeat with the remaining 2 dough pieces. (The biscotti can be made up to this point, tightly wrapped, and frozen for up to 2 weeks. Thaw at room temperature before proceeding with the recipe.)

Place 2 ropes on 1 prepared cookie sheet, leaving a good amount of space between them to allow the dough to spread. Place the remaining rope on the other prepared cookie sheet. Using a pastry brush, lightly coat each rope with the egg white.

Bake for about 30 minutes, or until light brown. Remove from the oven and let cool slightly on the pans on wire racks.

When still quite warm but cool enough to handle, transfer the ropes to a cutting board and, using a serrated knife, cut each rope crosswise on the diagonal into ½-inch-thick pieces. Place the pieces on wire racks and let cool completely. If the dough cools too much, the pieces will crumble when cut, so you must work quickly. If the dough seems too soft when cut, return the sliced cookies to a 300°F oven and bake for an additional 10 to 15 minutes, or until cooked through and crisp.

When the biscotti are completely cool, place the chocolate in a warmed bowl. Place a couple of sheets of parchment paper on a clean, flat surface. Working with 1 cookie at a time, carefully dip the cookies halfway and on the diagonal into the chocolate, allowing the excess chocolate to drip back into the bowl. Lay the finished cookies on the parchment paper and let stand for about 30 minutes, or until completely hardened.

Serve immediately, or store in an airtight container at room temperature for up to 3 weeks.

European Peanut Butter Chocolates

Makes about 19 dozen candies

Rather than just the familiar taste of everyday peanuts, this rich, luscious European-style candy has the added flavor of deeply toasted hazelnuts and almonds. The addition of bittersweet chocolate to the nut paste and the coating of milk chocolate make this a spectacular candy. It is a wonderful treat for a holiday dessert table or for bringing, beautifully wrapped, to a holiday party.

¾ cup sugar

About 3 tablespoons water

¾ cup plus 2 tablespoons blanched hazelnuts

¾ cup plus 2 tablespoons blanched almonds

3 cups unsalted roasted peanuts

½ cup plus 1 tablespoon cocoa butter (see Sources, page 192)

4 ounces bittersweet chocolate, chopped

2 pinches of salt

1 pound milk chocolate, tempered (page 13)

Line a large rimmed baking sheet (ideally a jelly-roll or half sheet pan about 13 by 18 inches by 1 inch) with parchment paper.

Place the sugar in a large, heavy-bottomed saucepan. Add just enough water to give it the consistency of wet sand. Place over medium-high heat and bring to a boil, without stirring. Add the hazelnuts and almonds and cook, stirring constantly with a wooden spoon, for about 15 minutes, or until the nuts are nicely coated and are a dark, caramelized brown. Remove from the heat and immediately pour into the prepared baking sheet, spreading out the nuts in a single layer. Set aside for a few hours to set.

Working in batches, transfer the candied nuts to a food processor fitted with the metal blade and pulse with quick on-off bursts just until chopped. As the batches are ready, transfer them to a heatproof mixing bowl. Set aside. Again working in batches, add the peanuts to the food processor and process until a rough, old-fashioned peanut butter consistency has formed. Scrape the peanut butter into the bowl. Set aside.

Line the baking sheet with a fresh sheet of parchment paper. Place the cocoa butter in the top half of a double boiler. Place over (not touching) gently simmering water in the bottom pan and heat, stirring frequently, for about 4 minutes, or until completely smooth. Add the bittersweet chocolate a bit at a time, stirring until smooth. Scrape the chocolate–cocoa butter mixture into the nut paste and beat with a wooden spoon to combine. Add the salt and stir to blend. Pour the mixture into the prepared baking sheet, spreading it out to an even layer. Set aside to set for at least 6 hours or up to overnight.

Pour enough of the milk chocolate over the top of the nut mixture to make a thick layer and smooth it with an offset spatula. This will be the top of the finished candy, so you want an attractive layer slightly thicker than the bottom layer. Set aside for about 30 minutes to harden.

Place a piece of parchment paper on the top of the set candy and carefully turn it out onto a flat surface. Pour the remaining tempered milk chocolate over the uncoated side, again smoothing it with an offset spatula. Set aside for about 30 minutes to harden.

When completely set, using a sharp chef's knife or a rolling cutter (such as a pizza cutter), cut the candy into 1-inch squares.

Wrap each candy in plastic film or a candy wrapper. Store the candies in an airtight container at room temperature for up to 1 week.

Chocolate Tuiles

Makes about 6 dozen

The curved shape of these cookies makes them a wonderful garnish for ice cream or other desserts. They are named after the traditional curved roof tiles (*tuile* is French for "tile") seen in France and elsewhere in the Mediterranean, and are easy to make except when it is humid, as the dampness in the air will cause them to wilt. You can purchase specially designed pans for making *tuiles*, but I find it is just as easy to drape them over a rolling pin or an empty wine bottle.

3 ¾ cups confectioners' sugar

½ cup Dutch-processed cocoa powder

½ cup water

¾ cup (1 ½ sticks) unsalted butter, melted and cooled

¾ cup plus 1 tablespoon cake flour

¾ cup chopped walnuts or hazelnuts or blanched almonds

Preheat the oven to 400°F. Have ready a nonstick cookie sheet, or line a regular cookie sheet with a silicone mat.

In a bowl, combine the confectioners' sugar, cocoa powder, and water and whisk until well blended. Add the butter and whisk just to combine. Using a rubber spatula, fold in the flour just to incorporate. Do not overmix, or the batter will shrink as the cookies bake. If lumps form, carefully break them up with the spatula and incorporate them into the batter. (The batter can be made to this point, covered, and refrigerated for up to 1 week. Return to room temperature before proceeding.)

Using a small offset spatula, spread the batter into circles about 2 inches in diameter and ⅛ inch thick on the prepared cookie sheet, spacing them about 2 inches apart. Sprinkle some chopped nuts in the center of each circle. Have a clean rolling pin or a bottle or two at hand.

Bake for about 10 minutes, or until just set. Remove from the oven and let rest for 30 seconds. Using an offset spatula and working quickly, lift the cookies one at a time from the pan and drape, nut side up, over the rolling pin. Allow the cookies to cool on the rolling pin for about 3 minutes, so they will hold their shape. If they cool on the pan before you get a chance to drape them, place the pan back in the oven for about a minute to soften them. Transfer the cookies to a wire rack and repeat with the remaining batter. Serve immediately, or store in an airtight container at room temperature for up to 5 days.

Chocolate Almond Chews

Makes about 8 dozen

These aren't really cookies or candy or cake. They are just deliciously chocolatey, nutty treats. Since they are tiny, they are a snap to pop in your mouth for a quick afternoon or anytime pick-me-up. Simple to prepare, quick to bake, and easier to eat!

1 ¾ cups plus 2 tablespoons almond paste

———

5 large eggs, at room temperature

———

½ cup Dutch-processed cocoa powder

———

½ cup plus 1 tablespoon unsalted butter, melted and cooled

———

Preheat the oven to 350°F. Lightly butter and flour miniature muffin pans or similar-sized flexible molds. Or, line the cups with paper liners.

Place the almond paste in the bowl of a stand mixer fitted with the paddle and beat on medium speed until softened. Begin adding the eggs one at a time, beating well after each addition. Add the cocoa powder and beat until blended. Then add the butter and continue beating until completely blended.

Spoon the batter into the prepared muffin pans, filling each cup to within about ⅛ inch of the rim. Bake for 8 minutes, or until just set. Be careful not to overbake, or the chews will dry out. Remove from the oven and transfer to wire racks to cool.

Layer the chews, separated by sheets of waxed paper, in an airtight container and store at room temperature for up to 1 week.

Chocolate Babka

Makes two 12-inch loaves

I wasn't familiar with babka when I was growing up in France, although the rich dough is similar to a classic brioche. It was not until I came to New York that I was introduced to this traditional eastern European bread, which I have come to love. I've added a layer of vanilla-flavored French meringue to the classic chocolate filling. It is wonderful for breakfast and since it will keep for a day or two, well-wrapped in a cool spot, you can slice it and lightly toast it to get the warm-from-the-oven sensation later in the week.

4 cups all-purpose flour

½ cup sugar

2 envelopes (2½ teaspoons each) active dry yeast

2 teaspoons salt

3 large eggs, at room temperature

½ cup plus 2 tablespoons milk

1½ tablespoons water

¾ cup unsalted butter, at room temperature

5 tablespoons heavy cream

3½ ounces finely chopped bittersweet chocolate

French Meringue (recipe follows)

Place the flour in the bowl of a stand mixer fitted with the paddle. Add the sugar, yeast, and salt, stirring to blend. Add the eggs, milk, and water and begin beating on low for about 5 minutes, or until the mixture has just begun to come together. Add the butter, raise the speed to medium-high, and beat for about 8 minutes, or until the dough pulls away from the sides of the bowl. The dough should be slightly sticky and wet.

Using a rubber spatula, scrape the dough from the bowl onto a clean work surface and pat it into a disk. Place the disk in a large bowl, cover with plastic film, and let rest for 30 minutes to begin the fermentation process. Then remove the dough from the bowl, completely wrap in plastic film, and refrigerate for 2 hours or overnight.

While the dough is rising, make the chocolate filling and the French Meringue.

Place the chocolate in a medium heatproof mixing bowl. Set aside.

Place the cream in a small heavy-bottomed saucepan over medium-low heat. Cook just until bubbles begin to form around the edge. Pour the hot cream over the chocolate and let stand for 30 seconds. Then, using a wire whisk, beat until smooth and shiny. Set aside to cool to room temperature.

Lightly spray two 9-inch nonstick round ring mold pans or two 12-inch nonstick loaf pans with nonstick vegetable spray. Set aside.

Lightly flour a clean, flat work surface.

Remove the dough from the refrigerator, unwrap, and divide it in half. Place one half in the center of the floured surface and lightly flour each side of the dough. Using a rolling pin, roll the dough out to a 12-by-15-inch rectangle. Repeat the process with the remaining dough half.

Using a large offset spatula, spread half of the cooled chocolate mixture over each dough rectangle, taking care to completely cover the entire surface. Cover the chocolate with an even layer of the French Meringue on each piece.

Beginning at the shorter end, roll each rectangle into a tight cylinder that will fit firmly into the ring mold or loaf pan. Place a babka, seam side down, in each pan. Cover loosely and set aside in a warm, dry place for about 1 hour, or until the babkas have doubled in size and risen slightly higher than the edge of each pan.

About 30 minutes before the babkas have finished rising, preheat the oven to 350°F.

When the dough has risen to its full height bake for about 40 minutes, or until golden brown.

Remove from the oven and place on wire racks to cool for 10 minutes. Invert the pans and remove the babkas. Serve warm or at room temperature. The babkas may be stored, tightly wrapped in plastic film, in a cool, dry spot for up to 3 days.

French Meringue

Generous ½ cup sugar

———

1 vanilla bean, split in half lengthwise

———

2 large egg whites, at room temperature

———

Place the sugar in a small mixing bowl. Using a paring knife, scrape the seeds from the vanilla bean into the sugar. (Don't discard the vanilla bean. Use it to flavor sugar or syrups for drinks.) Stir to combine. Set aside.

Place the egg whites in the bowl of a stand mixer fitted with the whip. Beat on medium speed for about 3 minutes or until the whites are fluffy. Begin slowly adding the sugar. When all of the sugar has been added, raise the speed to medium-high and beat for about 5 minutes, or until stiff, but not dry, peaks form.

Use as directed in the recipe.

Pain au Chocolat

Makes 24

When I first came to the United States, it was rare to find a good croissant, and I never saw a *pain au chocolat*. Now American children love them as much as I did as a kid in France. It seems that puff pastry requires some patience and concentration, but it is not too difficult to make. There is a lot of waiting time before the *pains* are ready to bake and eat. You can also make plain croissants with this dough.

1 cup (2 sticks) plus 5 tablespoons unsalted butter, at room temperature

2 envelopws (2½ tablespoons each) active dry yeast

½ cup plus 1 tablespoon water

3 ⅓ cups bread flour, or as needed

⅓ cup sugar

2 teaspoons salt

¾ cup plus 1 tablespoon milk

9 ounces bittersweet chocolate, chopped

2 large egg yolks, at room temperature

1 large egg, at room temperature

Lightly flour a rimmed baking sheet.

In a small saucepan, melt 3 tablespoons of the butter over low heat, then immediately remove from the heat. Set aside.

Combine the yeast and water in a small bowl. Set aside.

In the bowl of a stand mixer fitted with the paddle, combine the 3⅓ cups flour, the sugar, and the salt. Stir to blend. Add ½ cup plus 1 tablespoon of the milk and the warm butter and beat on medium speed for about 5 seconds, or just until the ingredients have mingled. Add the dissolved yeast and water, increase the speed to medium-high, and beat for about 5 minutes, or until the dough easily comes together and no longer sticks to the sides of the bowl. The dough should be soft and pliable. If the dough seems too soft, add more flour a tablespoon at a time until the dough firms up. If the dough seems too firm, add cold water no more than a tablespoon at a time until softened. Using your hands, gather up the dough, pat into a ball, and transfer the ball to the prepared baking sheet. Cover with plastic film and let rest for 30 minutes.

Lightly flour a clean, flat work surface. Place the dough in the center of the floured surface and roll it out into an 8-by-15-inch rectangle about ¼ inch thick. Wrap the rectangle in plastic film and refrigerate for 2 hours.

Lightly flour a clean, flat work surface. Unwrap the dough rectangle and place it on the floured surface with a long side facing you. Using an offset spatula, evenly spread the remaining 1 cup plus 2 tablespoons butter over the right two-thirds of the rectangle. Fold the unbuttered third up and over the center and then fold the right side up and over the first fold. The dough should look like a folded business letter.

Again, lightly flour the work surface. Roll out the dough into a 10-by-30-inch rectangle about ⅛ inch thick. With a long side facing you, fold the short ends of the rectangle in to meet in the middle. Do not overlap them. Then, fold one-half of the folded dough over the other half. Wrap the dough in plastic film and refrigerate for at least 2 hours but preferably overnight.

Lightly flour a clean, flat work surface. Unwrap the dough and place it on the floured surface. Again roll out the dough into a 10-by-30-inch rectangle. Fold the left one-third of the dough over the center, and fold the right third up and over the first fold. Again, the dough should look like a folded business letter. Wrap tightly in plastic film and refrigerate for 30 minutes or overnight.

Lightly flour a clean, flat work surface. Unwrap the dough and place on the floured surface. Roll out the dough into a 10-by-36-inch rectangle, taking care that the edges are straight. Using a chef's knife, cut the dough into 3½-by-4½-inch rectangles. Lightly flour another clean, flat work surface. Transfer the small rectangles to the floured surface with the longer side facing you. Place about 1½ teaspoons of the chopped chocolate on the upper third of a rectangle. Fold the upper third of the dough over the chocolate. Place another 1½ teaspoons of the chocolate along the seam of the folded dough. Fold the bottom third of the dough over the chocolate. Repeat to fill the remaining rectangles the same way. (At this point, the rolls may be wrapped in plastic film and frozen for up to 1 week. Thaw on a parchment paper–lined baking sheet in the refrigerator before finishing.)

Line 2 rimmed baking sheets with parchment paper. Place the rolls, seam side down, on the prepared baking sheets, spacing them about 2 inches apart. Cover lightly with plastic film and let rise in a warm place for 1½ to 3 hours, or until the rolls have doubled in size and are light and airy.

Preheat the oven to 400°F.

In a small bowl, combine the egg yolks, whole egg, and the remaining ¼ cup milk and whisk until well blended. Uncover the rolls and, using a pastry brush, gently coat the entire surface of each roll with the egg wash.

Bake for about 10 minutes, or until golden brown and just oozing chocolate. Remove from the oven and serve immediately.

If you have any remaining, wrap tightly and freeze for up to 2 weeks. Thaw at room temperature and warm in a low oven before serving.

DECEMBER

*Christmas, Hanukkah, Kwanzaa,
and Other Winter Celebrations*

December brings the culmination of our year's work. When we first opened Jacques Torres Chocolate, we had no idea of the magnitude of holiday business. As a pastry chef, I had experienced the festive season with overbooked tables and over-the-top celebrations, but never had I really known how much Americans enjoy gift giving. Their generosity is unheard of in other parts of the world. Boxes of bonbons, chocolate Santas and other seasonal icons, hot-chocolate mixes, and all kinds of chocolate treats are happily always at the top of everyone's gift list.

Growing up in France, the focus of Christmas was more on its religious significance than on the exchange of presents. I always left my shoes by the fireplace to be filled with little gifts of simple toys and sweets from Père Noël, but I had no idea that I could write him a letter that would result in my every wish being fulfilled on Christmas morning. Being a child at heart, I've tried revisiting the letter to Santa, but Kris doesn't buy it!

In France, children leave empty shoes by the fireplace for Father Christmas to fill with gifts. The shoes used to be wooden ones, called *sabots*, worn traditionally by peasants. Although leather shoes long ago replaced them in the fields, "wooden" shoes molded in chocolate and filled with candies are part of the holiday tableau in confectionary shops throughout France at Christmastime.

A *bûche de Noël* (page 174), or Yule log, is a French Christmas tradition that has made an inroad into American celebrations. A sponge-type cake known as a genoise, often flavored chocolate, is baked in a sheet pan; covered with buttercream, pastry cream, or whipped cream; and rolled up into a log. It is typically frosted with buttercream and decorated with meringue mushrooms, chocolate curls, or other extravagant embellishments. In France, it is usually enjoyed at the end of a bountiful late supper called *le réveillon*, which is served after mass on Christmas Eve. Even though I no longer spend my days in the pastry kitchen, I still make a *bûche* or two to include in our holiday celebration.

Chocolate-Covered Candied Grapefruit Peel

———

Bûche de Noël

———

Mendiants

———

Chocolate Marshmallows

———

Chocolate Bread Pudding

———

Chocolate Sauce

———

Peanut Brittle

———

Chocolate Diamonds

No matter how busy we are at the stores, there is one day that we all stop and take a break with chocolates and Champagne. December 20 is the anniversary of Jacques Torres Chocolate, and each year we feel blessed to have accomplished so many of our dreams. Friends stop by for a toast, and we all raise our glasses to the future.

Otherwise, we have little time to dwell on the spirit of the holiday season, as we try to keep up with the shopping needs of our loyal customers. During December, I often wish that I could find some Oompah Loompahs to work double shifts, just as they did in *Willy Wonka and the Chocolate Factory*. Boxes of bonbons are shipped all over the world, and everyone at the stores is busy late into the night trying to meet the demand for gift baskets, molded chocolates, and bonbon treats. But as busy as we are, we are always cheered by the expectant faces of children with visions of sugarplums dancing in their heads.

Chocolate-Covered
Candied Grapefruit Peel

Makes about 7 dozen pieces

A wonderful seasonal treat, these delicate candied peels are a nice twist on the more familiar chocolate-dipped orange peel. Instead of discarding the peels after your morning grapefruit, turn them into this delightful candy. I particularly love these with a cup of espresso after a rich meal. You can use this same method to coat other citrus peel.

2 large organic grapefruits, well washed and dried

———

2 ¼ cups sugar

———

13 ¼ ounces bittersweet chocolate, tempered (page 13)

———

Using a very sharp knife, carefully cut each grapefruit into quarters through the stem end. Working with 1 quarter at a time, insert the point of the knife into one end, between the flesh and the peel, and gently force the flesh from the white pith. Pull the flesh off, leaving the peel with pith attached. Set the peel aside. You can free the flesh in sections from the membranes and reserve them for breakfast or another use.

Cut all of the peels on the diagonal into strips about ½ inch wide. Try to keep the strips uniform, so that they will be attractive when displayed or packed.

In a large, heavy-bottomed saucepan, combine the strips with water to cover by 1 inch. Place over high heat, bring to a rolling boil, immediately remove from the heat, and drain in a sieve. Repeat this process 3 more times. This step is important because it pulls the bitterness from the peel.

Return the strips to the pan and again add water to cover by 1 inch. Add 1 ¼ cups of the sugar, place over low heat, and heat, stirring occasionally, until the mixture comes to a slow simmer. Simmer, uncovered, for 2 hours, or until the strips are sweet, soft, and translucent and the liquid has turned syrupy. Remove from the heat and set aside to cool in the syrup. (The cooled candied peel can be stored in the syrup in a tightly covered container in the refrigerator for up to 3 weeks.)

Line a large rimmed baking sheet with parchment paper. Place wire racks on the parchment.

Drain the cooled strips in a sieve, reserving the syrup, if desired, for sweetening drinks. Arrange the strips in a single layer on the wire racks. Let drain and dry for 4 hours at room temperature.

Place the remaining 1 cup sugar in a large bowl. Add the peel strips a few at a time and toss to coat well. Return the strips to the wire racks and let stand for a few minutes to set the sugar.

Lay 2 sheets of parchment paper out on a clean, flat work surface. Place the chocolate in a warmed bowl. Working with 1 strip at a time, dip the strips into the chocolate, coating about two-thirds of each strip and allowing the excess chocolate to drip back into the bowl. As the strips are dipped, place them in a single layer on the parchment paper to dry. If the chocolate is properly tempered and the kitchen is cool enough, the chocolate should harden in a few minutes.

Serve immediately, or store in a single layer in an airtight container at room temperature for up to 3 days.

Bûche de Noël

Serves 10 to 12

The *bûche de Noël*, a classic dessert of the French Christmas season, is quickly becoming an American tradition. Shaped and decorated like a yule log, the wonderful thing about this cake is that it can be as plain or as ornate as you like. You can make a simple log-shaped cake, cover it with buttercream, and call it a day. Or, you can make it, ice it, and decorate it with leaves, twigs, berries, mushrooms, little figures, and on and on. Here is the simple version that I like to make—chocolate cake, coffee buttercream, and delicate meringue decorations for a sylvan touch.

2 large eggs, at room temperature

2 large egg yolks, at room temperature

⅓ cup plus 2 tablespoons granulated sugar

1 ½ teaspoons whole milk

2 large egg whites, at room temperature

⅓ cup cake flour

¼ cup confectioners' sugar

About 1 cup Flavored Simple Syrup (recipe follows)

Chocolate Pastry Cream (recipe follows)

Coffee Buttercream (recipe follows)

Meringue Mushrooms (recipe follows)

Small block of bittersweet chocolate for shaving

Preheat the oven to 425°F. Line a 15½-by-10½-by-1-inch baking sheet (jelly-roll or quarter sheet pan) with parchment paper.

In the bowl of a stand mixer fitted with the whip, combine the whole eggs, egg yolks, ⅓ cup of the sugar, and the milk and beat on medium-high speed for about 6 minutes, or until the mixture is very light and has tripled in volume.

Place the egg whites in a bowl and, using a handheld mixer, whip on medium speed until foamy. (If you are lucky enough to have 2 bowls for your stand mixer, use a clean one and wash and dry the whip before using it for the egg whites. If not, the whites can be whipped with a handheld mixer or, if you want a workout, a wire whisk.) Add the remaining 2 tablespoons sugar a tablespoon at a time and continue to beat. When the sugar has been incorporated, raise the speed to medium-high and whip for about 5 minutes, or until stiff, but not dry, peaks form.

Using a rubber spatula, gently fold about half of the whole egg mixture into the egg whites. When almost incorporated, fold in the remaining half, taking care not to deflate the batter.

Place the flour in a fine-mesh sieve and, tapping on the side of the sieve, sift the flour over the meringue batter. Using a rubber spatula, gently fold the flour into the batter, making sure the spatula reaches to the bottom of the bowl to ensure an even mixture.

Scrape the batter into the prepared pan, and use an offset spatula to spread it evenly. Don't press down too hard, or the pressure will cause the batter to deflate.

Place the confectioners' sugar in a fine-mesh sieve and, tapping on the side of the sieve, sift the sugar evenly over the surface of the batter.

Bake for about 5 minutes, or until the cake just begins to brown on the edges. (The short, hot baking period allows the cake to retain its moisture, which will make it easier to roll.) Remove from the oven and immediately run a paring knife around the inside edge of the pan to loosen the cake sides. Place a sheet of parchment paper over the top of the cake, and then invert a cookie sheet over the parchment. Immediately invert the cake and the cookie sheet together, then lift off the baking sheet. Peel the parchment paper off the cake. Let cool completely. Line another cookie sheet with parchment paper. Place the cake on a clean, flat work surface with a long side facing you. Drizzle the simple syrup evenly over the cake, using just enough to moisten but not soak the cake. Spoon the pastry cream on top of the cake and, using an offset spatula, carefully spread the cream evenly over the cake, taking care to spread it evenly up to the edges. Starting at the long end farthest from you, slip your fingers between the parchment and the cake and begin rolling the cake toward you, up and over the pastry cream, until you have a firm log shape, or roulade.

Carefully transfer the roulade, seam side down, to the prepared cookie sheet. Cover with plastic film and refrigerate for at least 4 hours to allow the roulade to set.

Transfer the roulade to a serving platter. (Once you have decorated the cake, it is difficult to move, so it is best to work directly on the presentation plate.) Using a serrated knife, cut a 1½-inch-thick slice from both ends of the roll. These will be used to form "gnarls" on the finished log.

Using an offset spatula, generously coat the entire log with all but about 1 cup of the buttercream, spreading from left to right in long streaks. Place the 2 reserved slices on top of the log, positioning one at each end and a little off center. Cover the slices with buttercream, using the offset spatula to smooth the top of each piece. Pull a cake comb through the buttercream on the cake so that it resembles tree bark. Then pull the comb up the sides of the slices so that they resemble gnarls on a tree. Place in the refrigerator for about 15 minutes to allow the buttercream to set.

While the buttercream is setting, put the mushrooms together by gluing the caps to the stems with a dab of buttercream. Lay them cap side down until ready to place on the cake.

Remove the cake from the refrigerator. Using a sharp knife, carefully peel chocolate shavings off the chocolate block, letting them fall over and around the cake. Arrange the mushrooms around the cake. Serve immediately.

Flavored Simple Syrup

Makes about 1½ cups

1 ¼ cups water

―――

⅔ cup sugar

―――

2 ½ tablespoons Grand Marnier or other liqueur

―――

In a small, heavy-bottomed saucepan, combine the water and sugar, place over medium-high heat, and bring to a boil, stirring occasionally. When the sugar has dissolved completely, remove the pan from the heat. Transfer to a heatproof bowl and let cool completely.

Stir the liqueur into the cooled syrup. Use immediately, or store, tightly covered, in the refrigerator almost indefinitely.

Chocolate Pastry Cream

Makes about 2 cups

4 tablespoons sugar

―――

1 tablespoon cornstarch

―――

2 large egg yolks, at room temperature

―――

1 cup whole milk

―――

½ vanilla bean, split in half lengthwise

―――

3 ½ ounces semisweet chocolate

―――

Sift together 2 tablespoons of the sugar and the cornstarch into a bowl. Whisk in the egg yolks until well blended, thick, and smooth.

In a heavy-bottomed nonreactive saucepan, combine the milk with the remaining 2 tablespoons sugar. Using the edge of a small, sharp knife, scrape the seeds from the vanilla bean into the milk and then add the bean. Place over medium heat and bring to a boil, whisking occasionally. Remove from the heat.

Whisking constantly, whisk about one-third of the hot milk mixture into the egg mixture. Pour the combined mixtures into the hot milk mixture, whisk to combine, and return to medium-low heat. Cook, whisking constantly to keep the mixture from sticking and burning. Just before the mixture comes to a boil, it should thicken enough to coat the back of a spoon. As soon as the mixture boils, lower the heat slightly and continue to whisk for another 2 minutes to cook out the raw taste of the cornstarch and to allow the flavors to mellow.

Remove from the heat and strain through a fine-mesh sieve into a clean bowl. Cover with plastic film, pressing it directly on the surface to keep a skin from forming, and let cool to room temperature.

Place the chocolate in the top half of a double boiler. Place over (not touching) gently simmering water in the bottom pan and heat, stirring occasionally, until completely melted. Using a rubber spatula, fold the hot chocolate into the cooled pastry cream. Cover with a piece of plastic film until ready to use. If not using immediately, refrigerate for up to 24 hours.

Coffee Buttercream

Makes about 3 cups

*3 large egg yolks, at room
temperature*

——

*1 large whole egg, at room
temperature*

——

Scant 1 cup sugar

——

⅓ cup water

——

*1 ½ cups (3 sticks) plus 1
tablespoon unsalted butter, at
room temperature, cubed*

——

Pure coffee extract to taste

——

In the bowl of a stand mixer fitted with the whip, combine the egg yolks and whole egg and beat on medium-high speed for about 7 minutes, or until tripled in volume and very thick, light, and airy.

In a heavy-bottomed saucepan, combine the sugar and water. Clip a thermometer to the side of the pan, place the pan over medium-high heat, and bring to a boil. Boil for about 12 minutes, or until the mixture registers 250°F. When the sugar syrup is ready, remove it from the heat. With the mixer on low speed, carefully pour the hot syrup between the whip and the side of the bowl, taking care not to hit the whip as you pour, or the hot syrup will spatter and burn you. Continue beating on medium speed for about 3 minutes, or until the outside of the bowl is warm but not hot and the mixture is slightly cool.

Add the butter and continue to whip on medium speed for a couple of minutes, or until the butter is incorporated. Raise the speed to medium-high and beat for about 10 minutes, or until thick, smooth, shiny, and well emulsified. Add the extract, a few drops at a time, beating until the desired flavor is reached. Be careful not to overbeat, or the buttercream will be grainy.

Use immediately, or cover tightly and store in the refrigerator for up to 3 days.

Meringue Mushrooms

Makes about 2 dozen

*3 large egg whites, at room
temperature*

——

½ cup granulated sugar

——

1 cup confectioners' sugar

——

*½ cup Dutch-processed cocoa
powder*

——

Preheat the oven to 275°F. Line a rimmed baking sheet with parchment paper.

Place the egg whites in the bowl of a stand mixer fitted with the whip and beat on medium speed until foamy. Begin adding the granulated sugar a tablespoon at a time, adding it until the egg whites have increased in volume. Raise the speed to medium-high, add all of the remaining granulated sugar, and beat for about 5 minutes, or until stiff peaks form. Lower the speed to medium and continue to beat for an additional 2 minutes to incorporate more air into the whites. They should be very light and stiff, but not dry and separated.

Remove the bowl from the mixer and, using a rubber spatula, fold the confectioners' sugar into the egg whites, taking care not to deflate them and making sure you reach all the way to the bottom of the bowl.

Scrape the meringue into a pastry bag fitted with a ¼-inch plain tip. To make the mushroom stems, hold the pastry bag at a 90-degree angle and squeeze dime-sized portions of meringue onto the prepared cookie sheet. As you finish squeezing each stem, quickly pull the bag straight up so that you leave a little tail of meringue. Make as many stems as you will need, keeping in mind that baked meringue is fragile and breaks easily, so make a few more than you will actually need. (I like to make enough mushrooms so that everyone can have one when the cake is served.)

Make an equal number of mushroom caps by holding the pastry bag at a slight angle with the tip touching the parchment paper as you begin to pipe individual meringues into ½-inch rounds. When you have a ½-inch round, immediately stop piping and pull the tip straight up, leaving no tail.

Place the cocoa powder in a fine-mesh sieve and, tapping on the side of the sieve, lightly dust the mushroom caps with cocoa.

Place the meringues in the oven and bake, with the door slightly ajar to allow the moisture to escape, for about 1 hour, or until very dry and firm. If the meringues take on color, the oven is too hot. Remove the pan from the oven, lower the heat, and let the oven cool slightly before returning the pan to continue baking.

Turn off the oven and allow the meringues to cool in the oven for about 1 hour. This helps dry them completely. If you don't have time to do this, remove the pan from the oven and carefully transfer the meringue pieces to a wire rack to cool.

Store the mushrooms pieces in an airtight and very dry container until ready to put them together when you assemble the cake. (If making the mushrooms for another use, you will need some tempered chocolate or buttercream to glue the caps to the stems as directed in the recipe.)

Mendiants

Makes about 10

The name of these French confections refers to the four orders of Mendicant (beggar) friars whose habits are reflected in the four colors of the ingredients—almonds, dried figs, nuts, raisins—used to make it. There is also a classic French cake topped with this same combination of dried fruits and nuts on a chocolate base. This version, studded with spicy ginger and crunchy, complex cocoa nibs, is my homage to a French Christmas tradition.

These treats seem to be particularly good to have on hand during the holidays. A few, gaily wrapped, make a wonderful gift and are a great pick-me-up after a busy day.

1 cup assorted nuts, chopped

———

¼ cup light corn syrup

———

*10 ½ ounces bittersweet
chocolate, tempered (page 13)*

———

1 cup cocoa nibs (see note)

———

*⅓ cup assorted candied fruit
like ginger and orange peel,
diced*

———

Preheat the oven to 350°F. Line a rimmed baking sheet with parchment paper.

In a heavy-bottomed saucepan, combine the nuts and corn syrup over low heat. Cook, stirring frequently, for about 4 minutes, or until the syrup has liquefied and the nuts are evenly coated. Remove from the heat and, using a slotted spoon to allow excess liquid to drain off, transfer the nuts to the prepared baking sheet, spreading them in a single layer.

Place the nuts in the oven and roast, turning occasionally, for about 15 minutes, or until evenly caramelized and light brown in the interior. Watch the nuts carefully, as their oil and the sugar in the syrup can cause them to burn very quickly.

Remove the pan from the oven, transfer to a wire rack, and let cool completely. When cool enough to handle, break apart any pieces that have clumped together.

Line a clean baking sheet with parchment paper. Fill a pastry bag fitted with a fine plain tip or a parchment-paper cornet (page 18) about half full with the chocolate. Begin piping circles about 1 ½ inches in diameter and ⅜ inch thick on the prepared baking sheet. (Although not as neat, you can also pour the chocolate from a tablespoon and spread it out into a circle with the back of the spoon.) You should have about 10 circles.

While the chocolate is still soft, begin making designs in the top with an equal assortment of the caramelized nuts, cocoa nibs, and candied fruit. Work quickly, or the chocolate will set before the decoration can adhere to it. If the chocolate does harden, dip the nuts, nibs, and fruit in a bit of tempered chocolate and "glue" them onto the circles. Set aside for about 1 hour, or until the chocolate has completely hardened.

Serve immediately, or layer the circles, separated by sheets of parchment paper, in an airtight container and store at room temperature for up to 1 week.

NOTE: Cocoa nibs, which are roasted cacao beans broken into bits, are available from cake and bakery supply stores and many specialty food stores.

Chocolate Marshmallows

Makes about 19 dozen

There is nothing quite like homemade marshmallows. Used for topping cups of steaming hot chocolate, in gooey homemade s'mores, or simply for snacking, marshmallows are remarkably easy to make.

1 cup cornstarch

1 cup confectioners' sugar

3 ¼ cups granulated sugar

2 ¼ cups light corn syrup

1 ¼ cups cold water

3 tablespoons unflavored powdered gelatin

6 ½ ounces bittersweet chocolate, melted and cooled

Combine the cornstarch and confectioners' sugar and place in a fine-mesh sieve. Generously dust the bottom of a large rimmed baking sheet (ideally a jelly-roll or half sheet pan about 13 by 18 inches) with about half of the mixture. Set the remaining cornstarch mixture aside.

In a heavy-bottomed saucepan, combine the granulated sugar with 1 cup of the corn syrup and ¾ cup of the water. Clip a thermometer to the side of the pan, place the pan over medium-high heat, and heat, stirring occasionally, for about 15 minutes, or until the temperature registers 239°F.

Meanwhile, put the remaining ½ cup water in the bowl of a stand mixer fitted with the whip. Sprinkle the gelatin over the water and let stand, without stirring, for about 3 minutes to soften. Then add the remaining 1 ¼ cups corn syrup and beat on medium speed for about 4 minutes, or until frothy.

When the hot sugar mixture is ready, add it to the mixer bowl and beat on medium-high speed for about 5 minutes, or until medium peaks form or the mixture has reached its maximum volume. Add the chocolate and whip just until combined.

Pour the mixture into the prepared pan. Lightly coat an offset spatula with nonstick vegetable spray and lightly press on the mixture to spread it evenly. Lightly and evenly dust the surface with the remaining cornstarch confectioners' sugar mixture by tapping on the side of the sieve. Set aside to rest at room temperature for at least 8 hours or up to overnight. Using a sharp knife, cut the sheet into 1-inch squares. Layer the marshmallows, separated by waxed paper, in an airtight container at room temperature for up to 1 week.

Chocolate Bread Pudding

Serves 6

I love to make bread pudding with brioche, but you can make it with any type of firm, good-quality white bread you like. Some bakers remove the bread crusts, but I prefer to leave them on. If you use an unsweetened bread, such as a baguette, you might want to add a bit more sugar to the custard.

This recipe is for individual puddings, but you also make one large pudding. Assemble the pudding in an 8-cup baking dish and bake it for about 1 hour. It is not necessary to unmold a larger pudding to serve; simply spoon the servings into small bowls.

6 large whole eggs, at room
temperature

———

4 large egg yolks, at room
temperature

———

¾ cup plus 2 tablespoons sugar

———

5 cups whole milk

———

½ vanilla bean, split in half
lengthwise

———

8 cups stale bread cubes

———

8 ounces bittersweet chocolate,
finely chopped

———

Chocolate Crème Anglaise
(page 106) or Chocolate Sauce
(page 186), optional

———

Preheat the oven to 300°F. Lightly butter six 4-inch round baking dishes or soufflé molds. Place the dishes in a baking pan. Combine the eggs and egg yolks in a bowl. Whisk in the sugar until thick and smooth. Set aside.

Place the milk in a heavy-bottomed saucepan. Using the edge of a small, sharp knife, scrape the seeds from the vanilla bean into the milk and then add the bean. Place over medium heat, bring to a boil, then immediately remove from the heat. Whisking constantly, whisk about one-third of the hot milk into the egg yolk mixture. Pour the combined mixtures into the hot milk, whisk until thoroughly blended, then pour through a fine-mesh sieve into a clean container.

Put an equal amount of the bread cubes and chocolate in each prepared dish, taking care that the chocolate is evenly distributed throughout the bread. The dishes should be about three-fourths full. Fill each dish about half full with the custard, pressing down on the bread to keep it from floating to the top.

Pull out the oven rack, transfer the baking pan to the rack, then fill each dish to the top with the custard. Pour enough hot tap water into the baking pan to come halfway up the sides of the filled dishes and push in the oven rack. Bake for about 45 minutes, or until the custard is set but still trembles slightly when a dish is shaken, ensuring a moist pudding.

Remove from the oven, transfer the puddings to wire racks, and let cool for 1 hour. At this point, you can serve the puddings warm in their dishes. Or you can cover them and transfer them to the refrigerator to chill for at least 2 hours or up to 3 days. When ready to serve, run a sharp knife around the edge of each chilled pudding and invert it onto a dessert plate. If using, spoon the crème anglaise or sauce around the pudding and serve immediately.

Chocolate Sauce

Makes about 2 ½ cups

I always have a jar of this basic sauce on hand for late-night sundaes, a drizzle over fresh fruit when there's no time to make a fancy dessert, or for eating straight from the jar when I am hit by a chocolate craving. Be sure to use high-quality chocolate to make chocolate sauce, ensuring the richest flavor possible. If you store some in a plastic squeeze bottle, it can be reheated (either in the microwave or in a pan of hot water) and used to drizzle squiggly patterns on a dessert plate.

During the holiday season, make up a double batch and divide it among five 8-ounce gift jars for last-minute hostess gifts. All you need to do is add a label and a snazzy ribbon.

1 cup plus 2 tablespoons whole milk

10 ½ ounces bittersweet chocolate, finely chopped

½ cup plus 1 tablespoon heavy cream

6 tablespoons sugar

2 tablespoons unsalted butter

Place the milk in a heavy-bottomed saucepan over medium-high heat, bring to a boil, then immediately remove from the heat. Whisk in the chocolate, making sure that you scrape along the sides and bottom to incorporate the chocolate completely. Set aside.

In a small, heavy-bottomed saucepan, combine the cream, sugar, and butter over medium-high heat. Cook, stirring occasionally, for about 4 minutes, or until the butter has melted and the sugar has dissolved. Remove from the heat and whisk the hot cream mixture into the chocolate mixture.

Return the pan to medium heat and cook, stirring constantly with a wire whisk, for about 3 minutes, or until the mixture comes to a boil and begins to thicken slightly.

Remove from the heat and, using a rubber spatula, scrape the sauce into a clean bowl. Cover with plastic film, pressing it directly on the surface to prevent a skin from forming. Let cool to room temperature. It will be thick enough to scoop up with a spoon.

Transfer to a tightly covered container and store in the refrigerator for up to 3 weeks. Reheat when ready to use. If reheating in a microwave oven, place in a microwave-safe bowl and heat on medium-high power for 20 seconds, then check and repeat until the sauce liquefies.

Peanut Brittle

Makes about 2 pounds

Until I visited the Midwest, I didn't know that peanut brittle was traditionally an old-fashioned holiday candy. I just knew that I liked it. I especially like it with the drizzle of bittersweet chocolate that I've added here. It keeps well and ships easily—perfect for last-minute Christmas gifts, if you like making your own.

*18 ounces (about 4 ½ cups)
unsalted roasted peanuts*

———

*1 ½ cups (3 sticks) unsalted
butter, cut into pieces*

———

Scant 1 cup sugar

———

⅓ cup light corn syrup

———

¼ cup honey

———

1 ½ teaspoons salt

———

*2 vanilla beans, split in half
lengthwise*

———

*8 ounces bittersweet chocolate,
tempered (page 13)*

———

Preheat the oven to 300°F. Place 2 silicone mats or sheets of parchment paper on a clean, flat work surface. Lightly spray them with nonstick vegetable spray.

Spread the peanuts in a single layer on a rimmed baking sheet and place in the oven. Bake for about 5 minutes, or until very warm.

In a heavy-bottomed saucepan, combine the butter, sugar, corn syrup, honey, and salt. Using the edge of a small, sharp knife, scrape the seeds from the vanilla beans into the butter mixture and then add the beans. Stir to combine, clip a thermometer to the side of the pan, place over high heat, and heat, stirring constantly, for about 4 minutes, or until the mixture comes to a boil. Add the peanuts and continue to boil, stirring constantly, for about 5 minutes or until the mixture registers 310°F.

Remove from the heat and pour an equal amount of the hot peanut mixture onto each prepared silicone mat. It should spread out slightly on its own. Cover with a sheet of parchment paper and, using a rolling pin, press out the mixture until it is about ¼ inch thick. Remove the top piece of parchment paper and let the brittle set for about 1 hour, or until hardened.

Drizzle the chocolate over the hardened brittle, then let stand for an hour or so to allow the chocolate to set. Using a sharp chef's knife, cut the brittle into pieces of any size.

Serve immediately, or layer the pieces, separated by sheets of parchment paper, in an airtight container and store at room temperature for up to 1 week.

Chocolate Diamonds

Makes about 6 dozen cookies

Coated in sugar that sparkles like diamonds on newly fallen snow, these cookies are the perfect indulgence on a wintry day, especially when served with hot chocolate, a frothy latte, or a cup of tea.

Most cookie recipes call for all-purpose flour, but this one uses cake flour to ensure that the tender cookies will melt in your mouth.

1 pound (4 sticks) plus 3 ½ tablespoons unsalted butter, at room temperature

3 ½ cups sugar

1 vanilla bean

6 cups cake flour

¼ cup Dutch-processed cocoa powder

1 teaspoon ground cinnamon

Place the butter and 2 ½ cups of the sugar in the bowl of a stand mixer fitted with the paddle. Cut the vanilla bean crosswise into thirds. Split one-third in half lengthwise and, using the edge of a small, sharp knife, scrape the seeds into the butter and sugar. Reserve the remaining 2 pieces.

Begin beating the mixture on low speed, then raise the speed to medium-high as the sugar begins to incorporate into the butter. Continue beating for about 4 minutes, or until the mixture is very pale in color and fluffy.

Using a rubber spatula, scrape down the sides of the bowl and divide the mixture in half. Transfer one-half of the mixture to another bowl.

To the half remaining in the mixer bowl, add a scant 3 cups of the flour, the cocoa powder, and the seeds of 1 of the remaining pieces of vanilla bean. Beat on medium speed until well combined. Scrape the dough from the bowl into a clean bowl, cover, and refrigerate for 1 hour. Wipe the bowl clean with a paper towel.

Transfer the other half of the dough to the cleaned mixer bowl. Add the remaining 3 cups flour, the cinnamon, and the seeds of the remaining piece of vanilla bean. Beat on medium speed until well combined. Scrape the dough from the mixer bowl into a clean bowl, cover, and refrigerate for 1 hour.

Preheat the oven to 375°F. Line 2 cookie sheets with parchment paper.

Remove both doughs from the refrigerator. Transfer the cinnamon dough to a clean, flat work surface and, using the palms of your hands, form it into a rope about ¾ inch in diameter. (If necessary to make the dough more pliable for shaping, strike it gently with a rolling pin.)

Lightly flour a clean, flat work surface. Place the chocolate dough in the center of the floured surface. Using a rolling pin, roll out the dough about 2 inches wide and the same length as the cinnamon rope. Using a paring knife, trim one of the long sides of the chocolate dough to make a neat, straight edge. Using a pastry brush, lightly coat the top surface of the chocolate dough with water to help the two doughs stick together. Place the cinnamon rope on the trimmed edge of the chocolate dough and begin rolling the chocolate dough up and over the cinnamon rope to enclose it completely. Trim the other long side to make a neat, straight edge to finish the roll, and press together to seal securely. If necessary, brush a little water on the seam edge to ensure that it stays closed. If the dough is very soft, place the roll in the refrigerator for 30 minutes.

Place the remaining 1 cup sugar on a clean, flat surface. Lightly brush the entire exterior of the roll with water. Lay the roll in the sugar and then roll it back and forth to coat it generously. If necessary, add more sugar, as you want a thick coating.

Using a sharp chef's knife, cut the roll crosswise into ½-inch-thick slices. Place the cookies, cut side down, on the prepared cookie sheets, spacing them at least ½ inch apart.

Bake for about 15 minutes, or until just lightly colored. Remove from the oven, transfer to wire racks, and let cool completely.

Store, in an airtight container, for up to 1 week.

SOURCES

With the advent of the Internet, almost any piece of equipment or any type of ingredient a cook could want is now available with a click of the mouse. However, these are a few of the sources that I use to supply my kitchens.

Equipment

Bridge Kitchenware Corporation
214 East 52nd Street
New York, New York 10022
(212) 688-4220
www.bridgekitchenware.com

J.B. Prince Company, Inc.
36 East 31st Street
New York, New York 10016
(800) 473-0577

New York Cake and Baking Distributor
56 West 22nd Street
New York, New York 100110
(800) 94-CAKE-9
www.nycakesupplies.com

Sur La Table
www.surlatable.com

A Cook's Wares
www.cookswares.com

Ingredients

Jacques Torres Chocolate
350 Hudson Street
New York, New York 10014
(212) 414-2462
www.mrchocolate.com

Dean & Deluca
www.deandeluca.com

Ingredients and Equipment

The Baker's Catalogue, King Arthur Flour
Baker's Hotline (802) 649-3717
Monday through Friday,
9:00 A.M. to 5:00 P.M., Eastern Standard Time
www.bakerscatalogue.com

Wilton Industies, Inc.
(800) 794-5866
www.wilton.com

INDEX